HOW TO TEACH ADULTS

In this Series

Other titles in preparation

TEACH ADULTS

A practical guide for educators and trainers

Mary Howard

BA MEd DipAdEd

How To Books

Cartoons by Mike Flanagan

British Library Cataloguing in Publication Data
A catalogue record for this book is available from the British Library.

© Copyright 1996 by Mary Howard.

First published in 1996 by How To Books Ltd, Plymbridge House,
Estover Road, Plymouth PL6 7PZ, United Kingdom.

Note: The material contained in this book is set out in good faith for general
guidance and no liability can be accepted for loss or expense incurred as a
result of relying in particular circumstances on statements made in the book.
The laws and regulations are complex and liable to change, and readers
should check the current position with the relevant authorities before making
personal arrangements.

Produced for How To Books by Deer Park Productions.
Typeset by PDQ Typesetting, Stoke-on-Trent, Staffs.
Printed and bound by The Cromwell Press, Broughton Gifford, Melksham,
Wiltshire.

Contents

List of Illustrations

Preface

Have you ever thought how much time we spend each day learning and teaching without being aware of it? Information is beamed at us from all sources. Some of it we acquire, some we reject. Equally, we pass on information to others by telling, showing, guiding or acting as models.

Possibly our most important job is to act as role model for our children. From the day they are born they are involved in learning. We guide and encourage them, allow them time to practise, support and praise them, indicate we expect them to succeed, stretch their achievements to a more complex level and all this in a natural and relaxed environment. Most people don't realise that these are exactly the skills needed to bring about successful learning at any age.

This book sets out to examine these skills in the context of adult learning and to provide a grounding for more in-depth study should you need it.

You may be starting out in your teaching career or already involved in situations such as teaching crafts or sports in a recreational capacity. Perhaps you are a trainer in industry, the social services, the nursing profession, the emergency services or have responsibility for training voluntary workers or the disabled.

Presenting a short course of flower arranging in the village hall might seem a far cry from teaching literature or computing skills in a college but the basic principles are the same. The secret is to apply these basic principles to your own particular situation.

Most of us have attended courses for one reason or another – some of them will have been stimulating, enjoyable and productive; others will have been a waste of time and money.

So what was it that made the difference? To a large extent the skills of the teacher. This book will help you acquire these skills so that your teaching will be effective in terms of your students' learning.

Throughout the text whenever the male or female gender only is used the circumstances are meant to apply to both genders – sexism is not intended.

Mary Howard

Is this you?

College tutor
    Supervisor

    Training officer

Sports instructor
    Student teacher

    Health visitor

Volunteer tutor
    Mentor

    Fire officer

Aromatherapist
    Lecturer

    Nurse trainer

Demonstrator
    Chiropodist

    Literacy tutor

Police officer
    Vicar

    Youth leader

Social worker
    Manager

    Language teacher

Musician
    Writer

    Ward sister

Engineer
    Potter

    Flower arranger

Upholsterer
    Craftsperson

    Yoga teacher

Embroiderer
    District nurse

    Course leader

Nutritionist
    Physiotherapist

    Librarian

Dance tutor
    Doctor

    Resource technician

Yachtsman/woman
    Gardener

    Cook

1
Becoming a Teacher

DECIDING TO TEACH

Are you excited about starting to teach? Is the venue your local college, adult education centre, factory floor, hospital ward? Or perhaps you've been asked to pass on your knowledge or expertise to a group of interested learners attending a course in flower arranging, crafts, creative writing. Congratulations. Whatever the situation it's a worthwhile occupation.

But as the first session draws near your initial excitement at being asked may start to wane and be replaced by nerves. Are you beginning to have second thoughts? Well don't...help is at hand.

Try not to lose your initial excitement because with it comes enthusiasm and this will automatically be transmitted to your students.

Having been asked to take the class means that others think you are capable. Your main strength is your sound knowledge of the subject whether it is mathematics, yoga, cookery or car-maintenance. So armed with enthusiasm, a sound knowledge of your subject and someone who believes you can do it, why are you having second thoughts?

Because these are not enough. And you know this otherwise you wouldn't be reading this book.

THE SKILLS YOU NEED

What **skills** does a teacher need? You probably have your own ideas because even if you haven't done any teaching you will have been a student, so can make an educated guess. The following are a few of the necessary skills, but you can probably think of many more.

Teaching skills
As a teacher you will need to be a good:

- *organiser* – preparing and planning so that the lesson runs like clockwork

- *communicator* – ensuring that the material to be learned can be understood by your students

- *resource person* – a source of knowledge for your students

- *motivator* – providing experience that will encourage your students to want to learn

- *counsellor* – listening to students' problems and helping to sort them out

- *assessor* – assessing your students' progress in order to plan the next stage of their learning

- *supporter* – providing encouragement and praise when your students are losing motivation.

THINKING ABOUT TEACHING

As well as being aware of the skills a teacher needs, you have probably formed your own beliefs about teaching and learning. Before working through the book it would be useful to examine these beliefs.

Spend a few minutes thinking about them and then complete Figure 1.

Teaching is only one half of the equation for it needs to result in **learning**. But 'learning' means different things to different people. What does it mean to you? Make a note on Figure 2.

When you have worked through the book it will be interesting to see whether your beliefs about teaching and learning have changed or whether they have been reinforced.

WHO ARE THE STUDENTS?

Your students will vary considerably in appearance, age, background and motivation. They may be adolescents who have transferred from school to college to take or retake academic qualifications or to take the first steps towards their chosen career *eg* commerce, engineering, nursery nursing.

If you are a trainer in industry, the caring professions, the police,

Please tick the appropriate box.

	Agree	Disagree
Teachers are born not made.	☐	☐
The best teachers are the ones with the highest academic qualifications.	☐	☐
Extroverts make the best teachers.	☐	☐
Physical skills are easier to teach than thinking skills.	☐	☐
The teacher's main job is to give information to the learners.	☐	☐
A teacher should pitch the lesson at the level of the brightest student.	☐	☐
Discipline in the classroom can only be maintained by an authoritarian teacher.	☐	☐

Fig. 1. Examining your beliefs about teaching.

Please tick the appropriate box.

	Agree	Disagree
Learning requires the student to be motivated.	☐	☐
Children learn more easily than adults.	☐	☐
Learning is a skill.	☐	☐
The term learning implies that something has been committed to memory.	☐	☐
Physical skills are easier to learn than thinking skills.	☐	☐
Students need to be taught to learn.	☐	☐
We learn by experience.	☐	☐

Fig. 2. What does learning mean to you?

fire or ambulance service then your students will be members of your profession.

In hospitals and clinics many of the learners are members of the general public *eg*:

- mums-to-be attending ante-natal classes with their husbands

- diabetics

- heart patients and so on.

They are taught about their condition by nurses. Physiotherapists also retrain patients in the use of their injured limbs.

Classes or courses in recreational subjects are sprouting up everywhere and the students attending will be of very mixed backgrounds and abilities. It's not unusual to find the old and young, male and female attending courses in gardening or yoga, whereas a pre-retirement course would be attended only by people coming up to retirement.

WHO ARE THE TEACHERS?

Teachers of adults have a variety of backgrounds and experiences and they teach in establishments such as:

- universities

- colleges of education

- colleges of further education

- adult education centres

- industry

and those used by:

- social services

- the health service

- the emergency services and so on.

Their qualifications will be just as diverse, ranging from university professors with degrees and doctorates through lecturers with institute and professional qualifications, to teachers with expertise and skill in whatever they are teaching.

Some of them may have started teaching in a recreational capacity with few formal qualifications and then decided to study appropriate subjects and go on to take a teachers' training course.

CHOOSING A TRAINING COURSE

Training courses are available for most levels of teaching. Some are short courses designed for a specialist area, such as training the voluntary helpers of the housebound or the disabled. Such courses may have been requested by Social Services and provided by the adult education department of a college.

The emergency services have their own training courses in their own establishments and these courses are staffed by members of the profession.

Other courses are aimed at providing the teacher with nationally recognised qualifications such as those listed at the end of the book. However, courses are continually changing their titles and content so contact your local college or library for up to date information on courses available at a particular time.

CASE STUDIES

Sarah sets the agenda

Sarah Johnson has City and Guilds qualifications in cookery. She was asked by the head of adult education in the local college to take a cookery class on one evening a week.

It had been advertised as 'Simple Entertaining' and was to take place in the local secondary school.

On her first evening she started promptly by demonstrating seafood vol-au-vents, followed by a lemon souffle. Students drifted in during the first half hour and stood at the back of the room. Sarah ignored them and didn't address the group until she'd finished demonstrating.

'This will be the format of the lesson each week,' she told them. 'I'll demonstrate and then you can make what I've demonstrated.'

As the students hadn't brought any ingredients they spent the second part of the lesson mumbling amongst themselves.

Sam is enthusiastic

Sam Hughes had been made redundant from his job as a foreman at a large garden centre. At 55 he was finding it difficult to get another job. The head of horticulture at the local college asked him to teach basic skills to a small group of students with learning difficulties who attended college on two days a week.

Full of enthusiasm and anxious to start with the basics he said, 'First we must prepare the ground. Watch me and then you can have a go.' He started to dig. The students were distracted by a football match taking place close by. They wandered away.

'Come on, lads. Now it's your turn. You first, James.' James took the spade and the others returned to watch.

'No. Not like that,' said Sam. 'Give me the spade. Do it like this.' James watched and then had another go but with no more success.

Ray is confident

Ray sat in the library with the other three candidates awaiting the verdict of the interviewing panel. Each had a good degree in engineering but Ray was confident.

The head of engineering put his head around the door, 'Mr Benson, would you come back into the office please,' he said.

Ray smiled at the others as they congratulated him.

The chairman of the governors greeted him once more. 'We have decided to offer you the post of lecturer in engineering in the college of technology, on condition you undertake the teacher's certificate course we discussed with you earlier. Do you agree to this?' he said.

'Yes, I do,' replied Ray.

'Well that's settled,' he said. 'I hope you'll be very happy with us.'

'Thank you,' said Ray as he shook hands with all the members of the interviewing panel.

POINTS FOR DISCUSSION

1. How would you describe to somebody the difference between learning and teaching?

2. Do teachers with high academic qualifications need to undergo a teachers' training course?

3. How do you think teaching adults differs from teaching children?

2
Learning

DEFINING LEARNING

If you were to look at everyone's response to Figure 2 on page 16 you would see that learning is perceived in many different ways. Everyone's perception of learning varies according to their personal experiences. It would be useful to examine your own experiences to see whether they provide a clue to what learning is.

In order to do this make a list of some of the things you have learned in your lifetime.

Does your list look something like this?

- talking
- walking
- loving
- swimming
- riding a bicycle
- respecting others
- hating
- reading
- solving problems.

Now try to determine how you actually acquired this learning. Have you mentioned the following?

- memorising
- doing
- practising
- examining
- thinking
- observing.

Memorising
This involved you in studying the information initially, storing it

and then recalling it at a later date. This is how you learned to talk – by listening, remembering and then repeating.

Doing
You learned to walk, ride a bicycle and swim by *doing* it. It would be difficult to acquire these skills by watching someone else perform them.

Practising
This required you to repeat the skills once they had been mastered in order to become more proficient.

Examining and thinking
These are skills required in reading and problem-solving. You needed to look closely at something and then make decisions about what to do. They are not the only skills involved in problem solving and more will be said about this in chapter 3.

Observing
This involved you in watching the behaviour of others. Children, particularly, learn by watching their parents and often internalise the way they love, hate and respect.

Does anything strike you about the list above?

In all the examples it can be seen that you were *involved* in the activity of learning and were not just a passive recipient, listening to someone telling you what to do. You have, in fact, just been involved in some of these active processes, *eg remembering* your past learning, *thinking* about it, and *examining* it.

What is learning?
How would you now define learning? Spend a few minutes reflecting on what you have read so far and try to come up with a simple definition.

Learning is a process which enables us to do something that we couldn't do before we learned it. The process, as has been revealed, involves being exposed to certain experiences such as observing a situation, thinking about it, and then doing something.

A common definition of learning is: '*A change in behaviour (what we can do) brought about as a result of past experience.*'

HELPING LEARNERS TO LEARN

How did you learn?
There must have been times in the past when you have felt more likely to learn than others.

Spend a few minutes looking back and try to determine the reasons for these feelings.

Have you included the following?

• The teacher made the subject interesting.

• You wanted to learn.

• You needed to learn.

• The teacher supported, encouraged and praised you.

• You enjoyed learning.

• You were not anxious.

The teacher made the subject interesting
The need to make the subject interesting might seem like stating the obvious. But often a subject that is interesting in itself is made boring by an unimaginative teacher and vice versa. Observe how an imaginative teacher puts over her subject, analyse her technique. Does she adopt an unusual approach? Could you use a similar approach when teaching your subject?

You wanted to learn
This implies you were highly motivated. What was it that motivated you? Was it the subject? Perhaps you had always been interested in it but never had the opportunity to study it. Would success in the subject bring you status or rewards? Remember to harness this motivation in your own students.

You needed to learn
The need to collect qualifications in order to go on to further study, or for job promotion, might have spurred you on. Perhaps you needed to learn a skill such as catering or floristry in order to set up in business. Students who come to you with a need to learn will expect you to deliver the goods.

The teacher supported, encouraged and praised you
An important role of the teacher is to support her students – never allowing them to feel that they can't cope. There must be reasons behind students experiencing difficulties in their learning and they need to be identified and rectified. At the same time it's important that you encourage them to persevere and give praise when they succeed.

You enjoyed learning
Ensuring your students enjoy learning is another of your tasks. You can help by making your subject interesting, by nurturing your students' motivation, by supporting, encouraging, praising and guiding them towards success.

You were not anxious
There are many causes of anxiety in the learning situation. Children feel anxious and sometimes afraid, when they start school, move to another class or change teachers – it's fear of the unknown.

Similarly adult students may feel nervous when they return to study after a long period away. Often older people expect the experience to be as it was when they were at school – when traditional methods of chalk and talk were used and students sat quietly in rows. They feel threatened when asked to join in discussions, experiment, be creative or display initiative. You need to be understanding and supportive if your students are to adapt to a more relaxed environment.

What hindered your own learning?
There have probably been times when you have felt anxious, and afraid to ask a question in case others think you haven't understood. There may have been times when you have come away from a lesson feeling that you haven't learned anything.

Try to identify why learning was unsuccessful.

Some of the reasons will be the opposite of those in the previous list. They may also include:

- The teacher:

    – was boring
    – lacked interest in the subject
    – was unsure of the subject
    – was disorganised
    – lost me amid the terminology and jargon.

- The subject material was at a level that was beyond me.

The first list of reasons are not too difficult to put right. The teacher can make the lessons more interesting, get up to date with the subject, be more organised, simplify the terminology and explain the jargon. The second point relates to the way learning takes place and needs to be discussed in detail. This will be done in chapter 3.

TEACHING STUDY SKILLS

The importance of study skills

The main task of the student is to learn and one of the many roles of the teacher is to teach **how to study**. Often this skill is neglected because few teachers consider it to be their job – they only want to teach their subject. The main argument is that they haven't got the time.

However, in the long run it would save time. Students who can study effectively are more likely to be successful in grasping the material to be learned so it's well worth spending time on study skills.

Learning to study is most important if your students are to take an examination at the end of the course. But many of the skills such as note-making, using the library, speed reading and so on can be useful for anyone wishing to learn.

Study skills include such things as:

- organising study periods

- choosing the right venue for study

- using the library

- reading

- note-making

- memorising

- essay writing

- revision

- tackling the examination.

Organising study periods

- Explain to your students that an hour a day will prove more fruitful than a block of seven hours a week; psychologically it won't seem such a daunting task and something to be dreaded. Very long spells of study can be counter-productive as there is a limit to the concentration span of most people.

- Encourage your students to make out a weekly timetable such as the one in Figure 3 indicating where study-times will fit into their daily routine. Emphasise the importance of sticking to it, explaining that the need to keep on top of their study will act as a motivator in itself.

- If time is at a premium then it must be used to the full. Each study session can be broken up into smaller units – see Figure 4 for an idea of how to break up a one hour session.

Choosing the right venue for study

- A quiet place with a desk or table and somewhere to store books is all that is needed.

- A bedroom, away from the noise of the family, can be utilised – preferably with some form of heating.

- Reading books or making notes can be done on the bus or train.

- Don't forget to point out to your students that the library is an ideal place to study. It is quiet, warm, has tables and of course reference material to hand.

Using the library

Teachers tend to assume that adult students can use a library. This is not always so.

- At the beginning of a course arrange for a library session so that the librarian can familiarise your students with the lay-out of the library, the reference section and the cataloguing system.

- Set assignments that require the students to use the library.

Reading

To study effectively your students must be able to read for a particular purpose. Explain to them that:

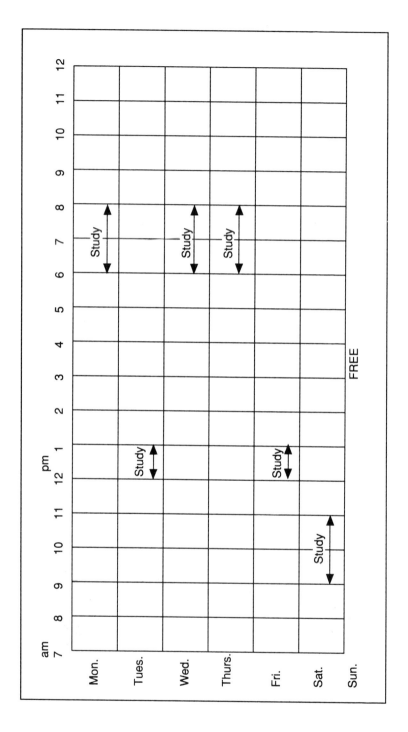

Fig. 3. Sample timetable.

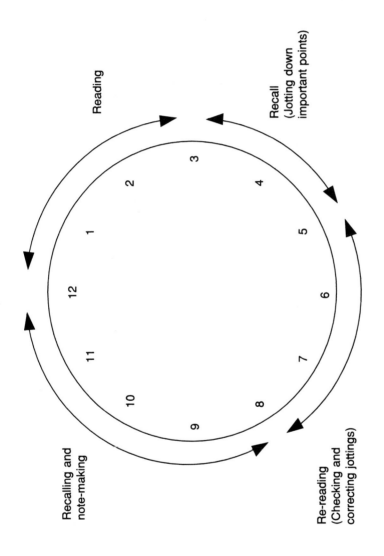

Fig. 4. One hour study period.

- It isn't always necessary to read a book from cover to cover.

- A general overview can be got quite quickly by skimming through the contents section, the introduction, chapter headings as well as graphs, diagrams and pictures.

- To master information a slower reading needs to be made and often repeated.

- As they become familiar with the book, reading to confirm knowledge or for revision purposes can be done more quickly.

Note-making

Being responsible for *making* rather than *taking* notes will ensure that your students are involved in decision-making about what to include and what to leave out. However, a certain amount of skill is required and you will probably need to:

- Give some guidance in the initial stages. This will be time well spent because it is a skill that can be utilised throughout life.

- Provide your students with a variety of methods of note-making that will enable them to experiment and choose the best method for them. If they've always made linear notes they may like to experiment with patterned notes or perhaps use a combination of the two.

Making linear notes comes easily to most people because we write in a linear form. However, there is a school of thought that suggests the brain absorbs and memorises information better if it is presented in pattern form, because the links in the information are more readily recalled.

If you aren't familiar with patterning see an example of pattern notes made on this section of the book in Figure 5.

Patterns can be made more meaningful by using diagrams to replace words and colour to highlight important areas. Don't forget also to use your own set of abbreviations. Everyone's pattern of a set of notes will be different and therefore only useful to the maker.

Memorising

Memory is an important factor in the learning process and students are always looking for tips on how to memorise information. Some

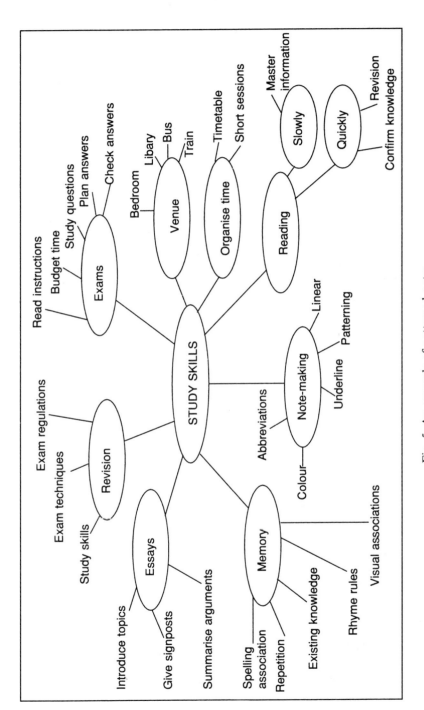

Fig. 5. An example of patterned notes.

students become anxious because their memory appears to be deteriorating with age, but perhaps it's just lack of use. The strange phenomenon is that they can remember quite clearly events of their youth (long term memory) but can't remember what they did the previous day (short term memory). It seems to be the inability to recall that is the problem, because given the appropriate cues recall takes place quite easily. With that in mind a session on aiding recall needs building into your study skills programme. The following suggestions may prove useful.

Making visual associations
Obseiving a variety of items and then trying to recall them is a game often played at parties. The secret is to link similar things together or pair things, like a knife and fork. If your students have to remember lists of items get them to visualise a location they are familiar with, for example their lounge.

Then ask them to imagine they are walking around the room and that there is one of the items to be remembered on top of each piece of furniture. The more outrageous the more likely they are to remember it. For example, when trying to remember a shopping list they could visualise a jar of pickles on the television, a bag of flour on the mantle-shelf and so on.

Using existing knowledge
Give your students one minute to look at the set of numbers in Figure 6 and then ask them to reproduce the arrangement.

4	9	2
3	5	7
8	1	6

Fig. 6. An example of a memory exercise.

Some will:

- try memorising them in the order in which they are presented

- link them to telephone numbers or house numbers

- realise that all rows add up to 15 and will only remember the numbers in the four corners and fill in the others as they reproduce the diagram.

Visualising the pattern formed by the odd and even numbers is another method of remembering them – see Figure 7.

Repetition
This is a method your students will be familiar with from their school days: remembering poetry or their part in a play. Repetition followed by self-testing can be particularly useful as an aid to memory.

Rhyme rules
Familar ones are, 'Thirty days hath September, April, June and November' and so on, or 'i before e except after c'. Encourage your students to make up rhymes appropriate to the material they wish to remember.

Spelling associations
Remembering how to spell words that sound the same but have different meanings, *eg* stationary and stationery can be remembered by associating station*e*ry with *e*nvelopes.

Essay writing
Many courses of study require the student at some stage to write an essay, particularly if there is to be a written examination. It could be argued that it's the job of the teacher of English to concentrate on essay writing, but your students may not be taking English. However, you can easily help your students with essay writing as you teach your subject, by giving an essay as an assignment.

Example
- Encourage your students to gather material appropriate to the essay topic.

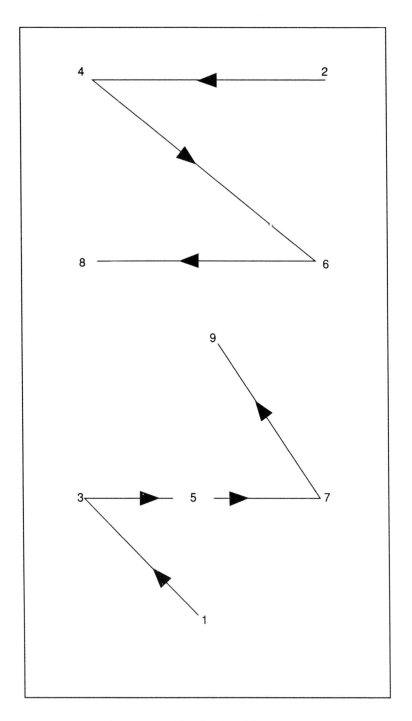

Fig. 7. Memorising by visualising patterns.

- Suggest they sort it and reject any that is not directly relevant.

- Give advice about writing the initial paragraph in which they will suggest how the essay is to be tackled and define any terminology.

- Explain the importance of giving 'signposts' along the way to keep the reader in touch with where the argument is going.

- State the need to summarise the main arguments of the essay.

Like all learning essay writing will improve with practice, so your students should be competent by the time they come to the written examination at the end of the course.

Revision

You will need to help your students organise their revision as they approach the examination. All the study skills discussed so far need to be employed and students who have mastered them should have little difficulty in revising effectively. It is also important to provide practice in examination technique and to familiarise them with the relevant regulations.

Although these will be stated clearly on the question paper some students are so nervous that they fail to observe them. They ignore instructions about:

- the number of questions to be answered

- the time allowed for each question

- the degree of choice

- the compulsory questions

- the question types *eg* essay, short answer or multiple choice and so fail to do themselves justice.

Tackling the examination

Emphasise to your students the importance of turning up at the examination hall in good time, so as not to arrive flustered. Advise them not to discuss the examination with other candidates before entering the hall. Hearing about all the topics they should have paid more attention to could make them feel depressed and dispirited. It's important that your students arrive feeling confident and they will if you have prepared them throughout the course.

In the examination room they will put into practice the skills you have taught them – reading the instructions and budgeting their time. They will be confident enough to spend time at the beginning studying the questions carefully and choosing ones they can answer well. They will plan each answer before expanding it in depth and allow time at the end to give all the answers a final check.

Advise them not to hang around for depressing post-mortems with other students.

CASE STUDIES

Sarah's students vote with their feet

Sarah continued to adopt the method of teaching that she'd used on the first evening. By the third lesson her students had dwindled in number to four and the dishes they produced rarely came up to the standard she expected.

'Are you sure you've been teaching your students what they've come to learn?' asked the head of the adult education department after she had told Sarah that the class would have to close.

'Well, I demonstrate different dishes every week so that they don't get bored,' she said. 'But to be honest they aren't very capable students.'

'Perhaps you're being too ambitious,' said the head. 'I think you might benefit from the teachers' training course offered in the college. I would be willing to provide you with teaching practice. Would you like me to put your name forward?'

Sarah accepted the head's offer.

Sam feels inadequate

After four weeks of trying to teach students with learning difficulties Sam was getting nowhere. He seriously believed they were unteachable.

'I've shown them how to dig and sow and prune but not one of them can do it. Either they are not capable or I'm just not cut out for the job,' he said to one of the tutors in the staffroom.

'We all feel like that at times,' his colleague tried to reassure him. 'I must admit you need a lot of patience but I wouldn't say they were incapable of learning. Perhaps you just need some help with your teaching techniques. There's a short course offered on Thursday evenings – 'An Introduction to Teaching Adults'. Why don't you join?'

There wasn't much Sam didn't know about gardening but his formal education had ended 40 years ago and so he was naturally apprehensive on the first evening of the course.

Ray starts his teaching career

'It's a doddle, this teaching lark,' Ray told his wife after the first few days. 'So long as you keep their heads down they're no problem at all. Plenty of notes and diagrams on the board for them to copy – that's the secret.'

'Sounds pretty boring to me,' his wife said.

'Learning is boring,' said Ray.

'When does your training course start?' asked his wife.

'Next week. I get a day off a week to attend for two years. From what I can gather I'm better qualified than some of them that are joining the course – they haven't all got degrees. So there'll be no problem. I'll sail through it.'

POINTS FOR DISCUSSION

1. Produce a simple plan of a lesson that you intend to teach. How will you actively involve your students in the learning?

2. Think of a lesson that you, as a student, felt was a waste of time. If you had been the teacher what changes would you have made to the way it was taught?

3. List the study skills that would benefit your students. How will you ensure they acquire them?

3
Analysing Learning

Can you list the skills involved in the subject you teach? If not it will be impossible for you to set up the conditions for successful learning.

English, maths, history and such like are often referred to as academic subjects while cookery, needlework and metalwork are seen as practical. But what is meant by 'academic subjects' and 'practical subjects'? Do they involve different skills and are different skills required to teach and learn them?

SORTING OUT HUMAN SKILLS

In chapter 2 you considered things you had learned in your lifetime. Do the items listed differ from one another in any way?

Examine the list and try to categorise the items. For example would you put walking and swimming in the same category, and if so why?

Do you have categories similar to the following?

category 1	category 2	category 3
walking	talking	loving
swimming	reading	hating
bicycling	problem solving	respecting others

- Category 1 items use the limbs and are often referred to as **motor skills**. However, when performing a task using the limbs the brain will also be functioning and making decisions about the sequence of operations, timing, speed and so on, therefore the term **psychomotor** is generally used.

- Category 2 items use the brain and are known as thinking or **cognitive** skills.

- Category 3 items involve the feelings and attitudes and are referred to as **affective states** that influence the learning of skills.

You could probably classify everything you have ever learned under these three headings. However, be careful not to assume they are separate categories because most of the skills learned will involve activities from two or even three of them. For example, driving a car is a complex operation involving not only the use of arms and legs (motor skills) but the brain as well (cognitive skills). Do you think feelings and attitudes are involved?

Feelings and attitudes are not things that you will set out to teach – they are acquired over a period of time and are a result of other experiences. We learn to have patience, to take pride in our work and to appreciate quality, while learning to perform a particular skill.

The late Arthur Negus on 'The Antiques Road Show' often displayed his feelings towards a piece of furniture by stroking it lovingly as he explained its history. He learned to appreciate (affective state) the quality of the wood and the skill of the craftsperson during his years as a cabinet maker.

INTO THE UNKNOWN!

Learning is a complex activity and there are differing views about what actually happens during the learning process. However, as suggested in chapter 2 learning will be hindered if the subject material is beyond the students' level of understanding. This is when they will say, 'You've lost me'.

Somewhere along the line there is a link missing between what is already known and the new learning. It's necessary to start from where the learner is and not from where you would like her to be.

Identifying where your student is, in terms of the particular learning, is an important task for the teacher. Learning proceeds from the known to the unknown, so it follows that the teacher must build on what the student already knows.

FINDING MISSING LINKS

The method of finding the missing link varies according to the type of learning. If one of your students is having problems in the cognitive (thinking) area of learning you obviously won't be able to see it. You need to ask her to *talk* you through the activity so that you can *know* how she is thinking and be able to pinpoint where the misconceptions lie.

If there is a difficulty with motor skill learning you need to ask the student to *perform* the task so that you can *see* what is causing the problem. Is she handling the equipment properly? Is the consistency correct? Is she applying enough force or pressure? As previously mentioned many tasks involve a combination of cognitive and motor skills, so by asking the student to talk you through the task as it is being performed, you should be able to identify problems.

It's important to identify problems and counteract them as soon as possible otherwise your students may become frustrated and give up.

This presupposes that you are familiar with the skills involved in the task and can pinpoint those that are causing problems.

ANALYSING TASKS

Example: threading a needle

Try writing down every stage in the performance of a simple task such as 'threading a needle'. Does your analysis read something like this?

Threading a needle (right handed person)
1. Cut the required length of thread.

2. Moisten the end of the thread which is to pass through the eye of the needle.

3. Take the needle in the left hand (eye of the needle uppermost).

4. Hold it at your eye level with the eye of the needle facing you.

5. Hold the moistened end of the thread in the right hand.

6. With the thread at right angles to the needle move the thread forward until it passes through the eye.

7. Remove the right hand from the length of thread and take hold of the moistened end which now protrudes through the eye of the needle.

8. Gently pull the thread through the eye of the needle.

The skills needed
A variety of skills are needed to carry out this task, such as:

• the motor skills of cutting, holding and pulling

• the cognitive skills of knowing right from left and the meaning of words such as, forward, protruding, right angles.

Without these skills (both motor and cognitive) it would be impossible to perform the task.

This might seem an over-simplification, and I'm sure many of you are thinking, 'But everyone can thread a needle'. Could a child of six months? No. The motor and cognitive skills have to be learned. Incidentally, try teaching a child to tie her shoe-laces – but analyse the task first.

Identifying skills
You will need to identify the skills involved in the tasks that you teach so that you are able to spot any that are causing problems for your students. This analysis needs to take place at the preparation stage of the lesson and the easiest way to do this is to:

• perform the task yourself

• identify every stage

• note any skills that may cause problems for your students.

Don't you sometimes wish the people who produce the instructions sent out with self-assembly kits were more competent in analysing tasks?

Activities
Try analysing one of the tasks that you teach. (In the same way as threading a needle.) It can be either a practical or cognitive task. Choose something simple – you will be amazed at the number of skills involved.

Now underline the motor and cognitive skills and consider what feelings and attitudes are involved.

Test the success of your analysis by asking someone to perform the task from it. Watch them carefully and don't give any other instructions. This will help you determine which skills they are capable of and which still have to be learned – also how perfect your analysis was!

Perfecting skills

Don't expect your students to be perfect in every part of the task at their first attempt – remember how long it took you to reach perfection. The important thing is to ensure they perform each skill to the best of their ability – precision and speed will come later.

You will need to supervise in the early stages to ensure that incorrect skills are not practised and so become habits. Short practice sessions will lead more quickly to mastery – long periods can be tiring and counter-productive.

There may, of course, be certain parts of a task that have to be perfect every time for safety reasons. For example, when nurses are learning the skills involved in giving an injection it's no use the tutor saying:

- You handled the syringe correctly.

- You drew up the drug properly.

- You cleaned the patient's skin well.

- You administered the injection perfectly.

- But there's one part of the task that needs practice – judging the *amount* of drug that you draw up. Your patient died!

Making judgements, of course, is a cognitive (thinking) skill, the others are psychomotor skills. Might there be attitudes involved in giving an injection? What about skill in reassuring the patient?

TRANSFERRING LEARNING

Many learned skills can be carried forward to new learning situations, for example:

- using machinery
- handling tools
- reading
- writing
- using mathematical formulae.

This is known as a **transfer of learning**. Teaching for transfer is what you should aim for, so that all learning doesn't have to start from scratch. Imagine having to teach your students to read before every session that required book learning, or how to use a screwdriver before every woodwork lesson.

EXAMINING LEARNING LEVELS

As you know some learning is more complex than others. It is therefore important that you as a teacher guide and support your students as they move from one level to the next. Much will depend on both the level they are capable of and their existing level. Remember to lead them from the known to the unknown.

Three levels of learning
Levels of learning are listed below going from the simplest to the more complex.

- *Knowledge* This is the term used to describe facts acquired perhaps from a book or another person. It is the sort of information that has been memorised at school, such as dates of famous battles in history. This information sits in the memory until it is needed, when it will be recalled. Once the facts are recalled they can be stated.

- *Understanding* Being able to state facts doesn't mean that your students understand the information. If they don't understand it they won't be able to progress to the next level of learning – that of application.

- *Application* Having 'knowledge' (information) is pretty useless unless your students are able to do something with it. They need to be able to apply it. But they won't be able to do this if they don't 'understand' it.

Example
Consider the cognitive (thinking) skills involved in the task of wiring an electric plug. Knowing the colours of the wires is not enough. Understanding the significance of them is necessary if the knowledge is to be applied safely.

Similarly, knowing the names of the parts under the bonnet of your car is of little use unless you understand their function and their relationship to one another. Without this understanding you would be unable to apply your knowledge to the task of solving the problem of why the car won't start.

Higher levels of learning

To be able to solve problems your students must have reached an even higher level of learning that will enable them to:

- decide what the problem is
- solve it
- judge whether it has been solved.

Sometimes, for one reason or another, progress is not made to the higher levels of learning. Some students with learning difficulties only reach the level of *knowledge* and this will probably have been acquired by rote-learning.

Example
When four such students were being taught to weigh out ingredients in a cookery class they knew what the scales should look like when they were in balance (neither side touching the table). They could repeat this whenever asked. The weight was put on one side of the scales and the sugar was slowly poured on to the pan on the other side until it hit the table with a thud. The students were unable to judge whether sugar should be removed or added in order to achieve balance. Their learning of the concept of balance had not progressed from the **knowledge** stage to that of **understanding** and **application**.

Assess your grasp of the levels of learning by giving one of your students a problem-solving exercise. Ask her to talk through the task as it is being performed so that you can assess the level of learning she has reached.

Teaching as problem-solving

You may perceive teaching as solving the problem of enabling your students to learn. If so, as with any problem you must produce a plan of action. The suggestions made in chapter 2 for helping learners to learn should help you do this. Consider the following rules.

Rules for learning

- Active involvement by the students, *eg* experiencing, reacting, doing, is more likely to lead to learning than passively listening.

- Learning takes place when it is satisfying a need and is useful to the students.

- Learning is more likely to be successful when it is at the students' level of understanding.

- The learning experience should lead to success rather than failure.

- Learning is more likely to take place when the teacher supports and encourages the students rather than dominates.

- The classroom should be a relaxed, non-threatening environment – anxiety inhibits learning.

If you take all of the above points into consideration when planning your lessons you will be well on the way to enabling your students to learn.

CASE STUDIES

Sarah realises her initial mistakes

For her teaching practice Sarah joined Marion, the teacher of the Cookery for Beginners course.

'This is my scheme of work,' said Marion. 'I discussed it with the group on the first evening and then adapted it to make sure it was appropriate for their needs.'

'I see you've started with basic skills and then developed them,' said Sarah.

'Yes. But it's important to ensure they've grasped those basic skills before moving on to the more complex ones. If they experience failure they become despondent and give up.'

'That's what happened with my students,' said Sarah. 'I decided on the agenda before I'd met them and the dishes I introduced were obviously beyond their capabilities.'

'Don't worry,' consoled Marion. 'That often happens. We forget we've been performing these skills for years. Try to think back to when you were first introduced to them. How did you cope?'

'Not very well, I seem to remember,' said Sarah.

Sam begins to see the relevance of the course

Sam soon lost his nervousness and found the teaching course just what he needed. There were several students of his age and he became particularly friendly with Brian, who was teaching students with learning difficulties in another college. They were able to exchange experiences.

'I hadn't realised there was so much to teaching,' Brian said. 'When I was at school we were shown once and that was it. If you hadn't grasped it, it was your own fault.'

'I'd never have guessed there were so many stages in a simple job like digging or pruning,' said Sam. 'I find myself analysing the tasks as I'm working at home in the garden. And to think I expected my lads to be able to perform a task perfectly after watching me demonstrate it once.'

Ray has difficulty accepting the demands of the course

Ray was beginning to lose some of his confidence as he realised the teacher's certificate course was more demanding than he had anticipated. All his preconceived ideas about teaching were being dashed. He was reluctant to change and made his views known regularly.

'The problem is,' he said, 'the majority of the group don't know anything about engineering – it can't be taught in the same way as English or history or hairdressing. Bunching all these different subjects together means that everyone's needs can't be met.'

'But everyone has the same need on this course, Ray,' said the tutor. 'That is to become a competent teacher. The course hasn't got anything to do with the subject you teach but the way in which you teach it. Once you know and understand what is involved in teaching you will be able to apply it to your own teaching situation.'

Ray wasn't convinced.

POINTS FOR DISCUSSION

1. Choose a task that you intend to teach. Identify the existing motor and cognitive (thinking) skills your students must have before they can tackle the new learning.

2. How will you determine whether your students have these skills?

3. Enabling your students to learn is your prime task as a teacher. How will you do this?

4
Understanding the Teacher's Role

In chapter 1, page 14, we see listed some of the skills required by a teacher. These will probably help you to define what teaching is.

Spend a few minutes considering these skills and see whether you can produce a useful definition.

DEFINING TEACHING

You will probably notice that in the list of skills 'transmitter of information' is not included even though many people consider it to be the main job of a teacher. The purpose of teaching is to bring about learning and you mustn't assume that by giving information to your students they are actually learning anything. They may well be but, on the other hand, they may not even be listening. Teaching must be designed to maximise learning – not left to chance.

To bring about learning in the classroom you must prepare in advance and the following points need to be observed.

Preparing the lesson
Make sure that you:

- organise the material so that you build on what your students already know

- plan the teaching methods that allow for student involvement

- analyse the tasks to be learned so that you can monitor your students' progress and ensure success

- allow time in the lesson for support and encouragement to keep motivation high.

In a nutshell then, teaching can be defined as: *providing the conditions to bring about learning.*

HELPING YOUR STUDENTS TO LEARN

In chapter 3 we suggested some ways to help bring about learning.

In this chapter we will look at these in more detail and consider how you could build each one into your own teaching situation.

> 1. Learners need to be actively involved in their own learning rather than passively watching or listening.

How will you plan and deliver one of your lessons so that your students are actively involved?

INVOLVING LEARNERS

You may argue that it is possible to learn some things by watching or listening. So it is, but there needs to be evidence that learning has taken place. All too often the teacher says, 'Do you understand?' or 'Is that clear?' and because the students nod their heads he assumes that they have grasped the new learning. But they may just be avoiding the repetition of information.

Choosing a teaching method that will allow your students to be actively involved is important but the choice will depend on the type of learning. (Teaching methods will be dealt with in chapter 5.)

Demonstrating a skill and then allowing time for your students to practise is an appropriate method for motor skill learning. However, if large-scale or expensive equipment is needed there may be insufficient pieces for everyone to practise at the same time. It is then that you need to plan alternative activities so that no one is idle and consequently bored.

Discussion and role-play exercises are appropriate methods for the learning of social skills but you need to plan and monitor them carefully if you are to be in a position to assess whether learning has taken place.

> 2. Learning is more likely to take place when the students can see that it is useful and satisfying their needs.

Do you know what needs your students have? Is it an examination or recreational class? Are they on day release or work experience?

How will you ensure that what you have planned is meeting their needs?

SATISFYING NEEDS

The motivation to satisfy needs can be seen at a very early age. The baby learns to crawl and then walk in order to get something he needs – a toy, an open door, the cat! As he gets older and goes to school he will become bored if he thinks that what he is doing is not useful or does not meet his particular needs.

Some teachers find it difficult to make the learning of decimals, sentence construction, photosynthesis or the wheatlands of Europe seem useful to a child. It is then that it needs to be linked to what they already know and preferably something they are interested in.

A boy well known for his dislike of school, his regular truancy and his inability to cope with arithmetic, had no problem working out his winnings when betting on the horses!

The needs of mature students
Mature students have different needs. Perhaps:

- They have missed out at school and welcome the second chance.

- They need specific skills to enhance job prospects.

- They require entry qualifications to higher levels of study.

- They have retired and wish to learn skills appropriate to their leisure time activities such as golf, gardening or crochet.

- They wish to attend purely for social reasons. The lonely, the bereaved, the overburdened parents who welcome the company and the chance to do something completely different for a few hours each week.

Whatever your students' needs, academic, job enhancing or social, they will look to you to see that those needs are met.

> 3. Learning should be carried out in an anxiety-free environment.

Are your students anxious? What might be the cause? Consider how
you will help to counter any anxiety.

THE CLASSROOM ENVIRONMENT

The social environment

Most learners feel anxious when they join a new class. They are
nervous about meeting the group and the teacher. Some are
apprehensive about the demands of the course and wonder whether
they will be able to cope. These feelings may be fuelled by memories
of past experiences.

Mature students will also have other commitments that must take
priority over studying, such as the responsibility of a family and/or
the demands of a job. These dividing loyalties will at times produce
anxiety. So what can be done to alleviate it?

Alleviating anxiety
Breaking the ice can be a problem. Some teachers ask the students
to give a thumbnail sketch of themselves to the rest of the group.
But being the centre of attention often increases the anxiety. One
way of getting round this is to ask them to tell their neighbour a
little bit about themselves and then get the neighbour to relay the
details to the rest of the group. It is not quite as intimidating giving
information about others as it is about ourselves.

This ice-breaking procedure enables members of the group to find
out whether they have anything in common. For example:

• Do they live in the same area?

• Can they share a lift?

• Have they got children?

• Do they have similar interests?

Adopting this procedure could provide you with useful information about the circumstances of your students. You may learn why
they have come – useful when planning your lessons.

They may have had to pluck up courage to join the class –
particularly if they have unhappy memories of school. It's
important therefore to respect your students and value their
contributions so that they develop a positive self-image.

Perhaps you have experienced the sinking feeling when homework has been returned covered in sarcastic comments outlined in red and you have searched in vain for a crumb of encouragement. Or perhaps you have suffered the embarrassment of being ridiculed in front of the other students for an answer that exposed your lack of understanding. If so then you will appreciate how important the attitude of the teacher is in creating an anxiety-free social environment.

The physical environment
The facilities of the room such as:

- size
- shape
- lighting
- temperature
- position

can all help or hinder the learning process as can the availability of equipment and resources. Is there an overhead projector and if so, is there a power point? This doesn't mean the better the facilities the more successful the learning. It is up to you to set up appropriate learning conditions with whatever facilities are available – that is what really counts.

Improving the physical environment
Quite often a lot can be done to improve the physical conditions of a room and make it more comfortable. Obviously the shape and size can't be altered but you can probably open or close windows and you may be able to adjust radiators. Tables, desk and chairs can certainly be moved so that they are not set out in rows with you facing them behind a desk. This is probably the worst arrangement for encouraging learning and certainly doesn't help produce a good social environment. The arrangement of the furniture, of course, will depend on the method of teaching that has been planned as will be seen in chapter 5.

Distractions
The physical environment can cause distractions, in that:

- The students might be so concerned about trying to keep warm or cool that they can't concentrate on the lesson.

- The seating arrangements might be such that they can't see the chalkboard or the overhead projector clearly.

- The dancing class or the music lesson going on in the next room may make it impossible to hear what the teacher is saying.

Whatever the distractions try to minimise them for they will surely interfere with learning and make it less enjoyable.

Whenever possible share the physical environment with your students *eg:*

- be part of their group discussion

- support their role-play exercise

- observe their motor-skill learning

- enable their cognitive learning.

This involvement will suggest to them that you are approachable and help relieve tension.

The cognitive environment

The *social environment* and the *physical environment* are both important in the promotion of learning, but so also is the *cognitive (mental) environment*. This relates to the interplay of all the mental processes within a particular learning situation, such as:

- The existing knowledge of your students which provides them with a mental preparedness for grasping the new learning.

- Your mental awareness of the students' existing knowledge so that you can plan appropriate new learning for the successful 'latching on' process.

When learning fails the blame is all too readily placed on the students but shouldn't the role of the teacher be examined as well?

An end of term report revealed that a student had gained 98 per cent in the physics examination. The comment was, 'Shows no interest whatsoever in this subject.' What an exposé of the teacher!'

> 4. The learning process should lead to success rather than failure.

Do you know why your students may not have grasped the learning you have planned? Can you make suggestions for improving the situation?

ENSURING SUCCESS

There are many reasons why the learning process is unsuccessful – the main one being a failure to build on what the students already know. There are others, of course, some of which were highlighted in chapter 2. But if the students lack the necessary foundation, learning can't proceed, *eg* we can't follow a map if we have no knowledge of the symbols.

Assessing what your students already know will tell you whether they have the necessary skills to be able to cope with the new learning. For example when learning to drive a car they need to be able to:

● engage the gears

● operate the pedals

● understand the highway code and so on.

Use of terminology and concepts

Another cause of failure to learn could be your confusing use of terminology and concepts. Because you are familiar with the terms related to your subject don't assume that your students understand them. Perhaps they have met them in different contexts.

A teacher of dressmaking asked the members of her group to 'baste' two pieces of fabric together (meaning 'tack'). They could be forgiven for appearing confused – most of them had only met the term in the context of 'basting the Sunday joint'.

Concepts can be either concrete or abstract. Concrete concepts such as, 'tree', 'vase', 'table' and so on are fairly easy to learn – they can be seen.

But the learning of abstract concepts such as 'easy' and 'difficult' often presents problems because the teacher can only give examples of them in use. She can't point to an 'easy' or a 'difficult' and misconceptions may lead to a total misunderstanding of the material to be learned.

> 5. The students should know what it is they are
>   expected to learn, not only during the course but
>   within each lesson.

How will you ensure that your students know what it is they are expected to learn?

OBJECTIVES FOR LEARNING

Students need a statement of objectives, setting out clearly what it is they are expected to learn throughout the course. This gives them a target to aim for.

These objectives may be laid down by an examination board or produced by the teacher at the planning stage of the course. It is, however, important that the objectives are the same for both you and your students if motivation is to be maintained. Sometimes students enrol for a course only to find that it isn't what they expected. Perhaps they wanted to learn conversational French but found that much of the time was spent writing grammar. To avoid this the objectives need to be made known to the students before enrolment.

In the case of examination subjects, the objectives provided by the board should be presented and discussed with your students at the onset of the course. Often innovative ideas for achieving the objectives can be supplied by them.

Using students' interests

Mature students have knowledge and skills that can be tapped and used to the advantage of the group. For example a student may:

- have contacts for an educational visit, to say a television studio or an archaeological site

- be skilled at using a video-camera and would be prepared to film the visit for discussion later

- have interests related to the course of study that she would be prepared to share.

It pays dividends to discuss the objectives of the course with your students because being involved in the planning of the lesson can be a useful incentive to learn.

The clearer you write the learning objectives the easier it will be for you to make an assessment of your students' achievements. An objective such as: *The students will know how to punctuate sentences* is much too general. It would be difficult to assess whether it had been achieved in the form it is written. It is a cognitive (thinking) skill, therefore the teacher can't see what the students 'know'.

She needs to ask them to punctuate some sentences so that she has evidence that they 'know'. The objective could just as easily have been written as follows: *The students will punctuate the given sentences by placing commas, full stops and question marks in the appropriate places.* The assignment could then be assessed more objectively.

> 6. The students should be able to cope with the level of learning.

How will you plan learning that is appropriate for your students' level of ability?

PLANNING FOR ALL LEARNING LEVELS

Much of what has been discussed so far needs to be considered when planning learning at the appropriate level for your students. It is your task to assess their existing capabilities and to plan the new learning so that it can be linked to what they already know. It is too easy to say, 'But they don't know anything about this topic at all'. With a little imagination something can be found that can be related to the new learning. For example, a nurse tutor about to introduce pre-nursing students to the skeletal system asked them to bend their fingers and toes to enable them to determine the number of bones in each digit.

Remember, don't tell, try always to enable your students to take responsibility for their own learning.

> 7. Students need a knowledge of progress.

From what sources will your students receive feedback?

RECEIVING FEEDBACK

It is important that your students receive regular 'feedback' regarding their progress. Delayed feedback, such as not handing back marked work for several weeks, is of little value. The interim learning will have been completed without any knowledge of results and therefore they will have no standard to work to. This feedback enables you to evaluate your students' existing capabilities and so help you with future planning.

Providing positive feedback, such as praising your students' good work, will motivate them to continue to strive to produce good work.

Sources of feedback

Students get feedback from the following sources:

The teacher
Probably the most useful source because she is able to discuss progress and provide the support and encouragement necessary to achieve the learning objectives.

Other students
During discussions or role-play exercises a student will get feedback about her own knowledge, understanding and attitudes from other members of the group.

The task in hand
A student can usually tell whether she is performing a skill correctly. Failure to do so will lead to a poor product in the case of motor-skill learning and perplexity in the case of cognitive learning.

---

8. Each stage should be mastered before moving to the next.

How will you ensure your students have mastered one stage before going on to the next stage of learning?

PROGRESSING SLOWLY

Assessing each stage of learning will enable both you and your students to decide on readiness to move on.

In the case of motor-skill learning the complete task needs to be practised until it is mastered. But it is important to ensure that each skill is being performed correctly – because practice leads to habit. Learning new skills from scratch can be easier than getting rid of bad habits previously learned.

Perfect mastery, as was mentioned earlier, is essential in some cases for safety reasons (remember the nurse drawing up the drug in the syringe?). It also needs to be achieved before using dangerous equipment. The students must not only have the knowledge, understanding and practical skill to use the equipment safely, but also the physical ability.

Supporting your students through the various stages of learning, ensuring they are competent to move from one stage to the next and then gradually withdrawing your support as they become capable of taking responsibility for their own learning, is your major task. Remember the greatest compliment your students can pay you is to, eventually, be able to do without you.

CASE STUDIES

Sarah observes how to meet the students' needs

Marion's class was relaxed. The students were friendly towards Sarah with none of the nervousness she had encountered in her own students. She realised this was a consequence of Marion's approach.

Before each lesson Marion provided Sarah with a copy of the lesson plan so that she could see what form the lesson would take.

'Was it your idea to demonstrate one week and allow your students to practise the following week?' Sarah asked.

'No. The students prefer that method. It has its advantages,' said Marion. 'It enables them to see the finished dishes before they buy their ingredients. We can then discuss whether they want to make larger or smaller quantities depending on the size of their family.'

'What happens if some students finish before others? How do you prevent them from becoming bored?' asked Sarah, remembering what she had learned on her training course.

'I always make a variety of dishes to show the skill being learned and they can choose which to make the following week. During my demonstration I also suggest how the dishes can be made more elaborate so that the more able students can experiment. You'll find that they quickly become aware of their own capabilities and they will choose the dishes they know they can complete within the lesson. This gives me time to discuss their progress and sort out any problems.'

Sarah could see that this system was meeting everyone's needs.

Sam gets some useful tips

Sam asked one of his colleagues at the college if he could observe one of his lessons. The tutor was delighted.

It was a craft class and the students with learning difficulties were making stools.

'You can help us if you like,' said the tutor. 'We're always glad of another pair of hands, aren't we lads?'

The students welcomed Sam with open arms – it was the least formal classroom Sam had come across.

As Sam helped Raymond sand down the legs of a stool, he noticed the tutor – with a specially devised ruler – helping Kathy to measure a piece of wood 30 centimetres long, from which to cut a leg.

'Come on, Raymond. Time for you to measure a leg,' shouted the tutor. Raymond eagerly moved over to him. Kathy was left to try to put into practice what she had previously achieved with the tutor.

After the lesson Sam said, 'I can see that having a variety of tasks helps keep them happy.'

'That's important,' said the tutor, 'but they need to be carefully monitored to ensure that the skills involved in the tasks are within their capabilities. I incorporate number recognition into the measuring session. They have to mark out 30 centimetres for the length of leg but many of them are able to transfer that learning to the measuring of smaller lengths of wood.'

Sam was left wondering how he could transfer what he had just learned to his own teaching situation.

Ray has problems

After four weeks of copying notes from the board Ray's students were given a test. They all did badly and Ray was sent for by his head of department.

'What happened? We've never had such poor results,' said the head. 'These are second-year students and all did reasonably well in their phase tests last year.'

'They're just not committed,' said Ray. 'They've had all the notes – it's obvious they haven't even read them.'

'Notes are useless unless they understand them and can apply them and that's where you come in.' The head had suspected for some time that Ray wasn't pulling his weight and these results were the last straw. 'How are you coping on your training course?' he asked.

'Oh, it's useless. It has nothing to do with engineering.'

'I'm surprised you expected it would have. You've already got the engineering qualifications, what you need now are the skills to teach. One of the tutors on the course has an engineering background, I suggest you go and see him – perhaps he can sort out your problem before it's too late. Remember you're still on probation in this job.'

Ray slunk out of the office resenting the implication that he had problems.

POINTS FOR DISCUSSION

1. What decisions does a teacher need to make before meeting a group of students for the first time?

2. What advice would you give to a new teacher who finds that her students are not grasping the new learning?

3. How will you ensure that the atmosphere in your classroom is friendly and relaxed?

5
Teaching Methods

The teaching method is the way in which the material to be learned is presented to the students. But sometimes methods are confused with resources. Such things as the chalkboard, the model and the film are resources that support the chosen teaching methods and as such will be dealt with in chapter 6.

There are dozens of tried and tested methods but you don't have to adopt any one of them. On the contrary, sometimes it pays to be innovative, using methods that intrigue your students and provide just the spark needed to fire their interest and enthusiasm. As long as your method achieves its objective (that of bringing about the desired learning) go ahead and experiment.

One way of experimenting is to examine the conventional methods and then adapt them to your own teaching situation. For example, a nutritionist listed on the chalkboard the nutrients contained in food and the students dutifully copied them down. They were obviously bored.

But their interest was recaptured as she slowly peeled an orange. What was she going to do with it? Was she going to share it? She started to eat and they watched. 'Mm, it's lovely and sweet,' she said as the juice dripped down her chin. Then she made a big show of chewing the membrane.

The students were asked to look at the list on the board and try to guess some of the nutrients contained in the orange. Needless to say they guessed:

- **Water** – from the way the juice flowed, and therefore the water soluble vitamin C.

- **Sugar** – because she had indicated it was sweet.

- **Roughage** – from the way she chewed on the membrane.

This exercise had provided a starting point for the teaching of nutrition and more importantly captured the students' interest.

Consider the teaching methods that you have experienced as a learner or used as a teacher. How successful were they in terms of achieving the required learning?

NAMING THE METHODS

It is important that your students are actively involved in their own learning. Do the methods that you have experienced make provision for this? Methods that allow the students some or total involvement in their own learning are called *learner-centred* as opposed to *teacher-centred* where the teacher is in complete control.

Figure 8 lists a few of the teaching methods more commonly used. They have been named either learner-centred (with the teacher acting as a resource person) or teacher-centred or a combination of the two.

Some of the methods are more useful than others in terms of bringing about learning.

Of course with project work the teacher will be involved at some stage – this will be discussed later.

PINPOINTING THEIR USEFULNESS

Using Figure 9 suggest points for and against using the teaching methods listed.

Lecture

The lecture is a formal method of giving information – usually by a specialist in the subject. It is a one-way method of communication.

Points in favour of the method:
- Once prepared it can be used on many occasions if the learning objectives are the same.

- A good lecturer can inspire the students with his/her enthusiasm.

- A large amount of information can be presented in the minimum amount of time, therefore it is appropriate for intelligent, highly motivated students.

- It is economical with staff time – it can cater for large audiences.

TEACHING METHODS

Lecture	Teacher centred (learner is passive)
Discussion	Teacher/learner centred
Project work	Learner centred
Note-taking	Teacher centred
Note-making	Learner centred
Demonstration	Teacher centred
Demonstration/practice	Teacher/learner centred

Fig. 8. Some commonly used teaching methods.

	Points for	Points against
Lecture		
Discussion		
Project work		
Note-taking		
Note-making		
Demonstration		
Demonstration /practice		

Fig. 9. Your assessment of teaching methods.

Points against the method
- It is limited to the giving of information.

- There is no student participation therefore misunderstandings are not dealt with.

- The student is a passive recipient and can easily switch off.

- Audiences are often large and unknown to the lecturer so pitching the lecture at an appropriate level is difficult.

- There is no ongoing means of assessing the learning that is taking place.

- Students must have the ability to concentrate and make notes.

Discussion
A discussion, used as a teaching method, is the discourse between a group of students (or students and teacher). It is useful for exploring and evaluating ideas related to the learning objectives.

Points in favour of the method
- Group members pool knowledge and learn from one another.

- No special equipment is needed, unless ideas are to be recorded.

- It can help develop relationships – group members work together as a team.

- People often contribute in small, informal groups who normally hesitate in large, formal situations.

- It fosters cognitive (thinking) learning and attitude formation.

- The group and the teacher become aware of the members' knowledge and attitudes so that misconceptions about a topic under discussion can be corrected.

- It may introduce members to topics that they will wish to study further.

Points against the method
- The topic for discussion needs to be chosen with the students' previous knowledge in mind otherwise some may be unable to contribute.

- It needs to be carefully controlled otherwise
  - it could end up as an unstructured debate
  - the extrovert members of the group may dominate
  - less articulate members may opt out
  - it could be time-wasting if allowed to wander from the topic.

- Some students may lack the ability to evaluate the information being produced and so be subjected to irrational attitude changes.

Project work
Basically this is a problem-solving situation which involves the students in finding the solution.

Points in favour of the method
- The students enjoy the freedom of taking responsibility for their own learning.

- They are given the opportunity to choose between material that is required and that which is not (a cognitive skill).

- It can incorporate motor-skill learning and the development of affective states such as enthusiasm, curiosity, perseverance and so on.

- A group project enables a large amount of information to be collected and used.

- Students experience working together as a team.

Points against the method
- It is time consuming for the teacher. She has to:
  - choose the strategy
  - produce appropriate resources for the students, such as reference material
  - outline a timetable for research
  - decide on a deadline for completion
  - monitor the work at regular intervals

– deal with problems immediately
– guide the students towards collating and evaluating the work produced.

• The students must have the necessary skills for 'enquiry'.

• It can be time wasting if not carefully monitored by the teacher – and the students will lose motivation if left to flounder.

Note-taking
This is confined to:

1. the recording of a lecture or dictated notes

2. copying notes from books, the chalkboard or the overhead projector.

Points in favour of the method
• Making notes while listening to the teacher or looking at the book, chalkboard or overhead project keeps the students busy.

• It provides the students with a set of notes for revision purposes.

Points against the method
• It can be a total waste of time in terms of learning, as the students may not even be thinking about what they are writing. (Why not give them a handout and use the time saved more fruitfully?)

• Many students find it difficult to listen and write at the same time.

Note-making
This is a cognitive (thinking) skill requiring the student to listen, identify only the information that is important and then organise it in appropriate note form.

Points in favour of the method
• The students must concentrate in order to understand the information being presented.

• Making only outline notes allows the students more time to listen intelligently.

- The important points are easily remembered for recall at a later date.

- Headings and subheadings leave plenty of room for expansion after the lecture – this helps consolidation of learning.

- This consolidation will enable the student to perform at a higher level of learning than the simple churning out of facts.

Points against the method
- The weakness is not in the method but rather in the students' inability to make notes rather than take them.

Demonstration
This teaching method refers to the performance plus an explanation by the teacher of the task to be learned.

Points in favour of the method
- The students have the opportunity of seeing a skilled performance.

- It cuts out a certain amount of trial and error learning as the teacher explains how to perform the subskills. (This leads to economy in time and also money if expensive materials are to be used.)

- A dynamic performance will almost certainly motivate students to want to 'have a go'.

Points against the method
- It requires a great deal of preparation and possibly expense.

- It may need specialist equipment.

- The teacher must be a skilled performer if it is to be successful and she must be capable of analysing the task to be demonstrated so that each skill can be shown and explained.

- If the students are facing the demonstrator then the task is being observed the wrong way round.

- Observing a skilled performance does not provide the students with the ability to perform the task. (It would be difficult to learn to plaster a wall by watching someone else do it.)

The demonstration of a task must be followed by practice – preferably immediately following the demonstration, while it is fresh in the students' minds.

Practice
This is the performance, by the students, of a task previously demonstrated by the teacher.

Points in favour of the method
- The teacher can assess whether her demonstration has been successful in terms of the students' ability to perform the task.

- Incorrect movements can be corrected before they become habits.

- With continued practice of the correct movements the student will be able to produce a polished performance.

- Once the student becomes proficient she will be motivated to transfer the learned skills to other projects.

Points against the method
- The teacher must be capable of pinpointing those parts of the task that are causing the students' problems.

- Without this feedback the students will continually encounter problems, resulting in loss of motivation.

- Continuous unsuccessful performance will result in habits that are difficult to break.

There are a number of variations in the Demonstration/Practice method of teaching and the choice will depend, to a large extent, on the ability of your students.

Some students will be capable of observing a lengthy demonstration in its entirety before practice. With less capable students it may be more beneficial, in terms of learning, to demonstrate a skill in stages – allowing them to complete one stage before demonstrating the next.

Very slow learners are probably better following the method of

'All do this with me now,' which enables them to 'copy' every part of the task as you demonstrate – they don't have to rely on memory.

Some tasks have, of necessity, to be demonstrated in stages. For example, a cookery demonstration will probably require the teacher to demonstrate one stage and place the food to cook for a period of time before performing the next stage. During this time the students can complete their first stage.

The above teaching methods have been dealt with individually but it is most unlikely that a lesson would be conducted using only one method throughout.

CHOOSING THE METHOD

The choice of combination of methods relies on several factors.

1. The type of learning to be achieved (motor or cognitive). For example the lecture method would be of little use in enabling someone to ride a bicycle. A demonstration (without practice) would only achieve the cognitive elements of the skill *ie* a *knowledge* of the skills involved. It would not enable the learner to become proficient at the motor skills such as balance, pedalling, steering, braking and so on.

2. The students' ability (related to the task being learned). It would be timewasting to set students a project if they were unable to read, use the library, and collect appropriate information.

3. The need to:

   • actively involve the students

   • keep the students interested

   • make the best use of the learning environment and so on.

To use the same teaching method throughout the lesson could lead to your students becoming bored – a combination of methods needs to be used.

Example: combining methods

A typical lesson might start with a short **lecture** introducing the learning objectives followed by a **discussion** on how best to achieve them. This could lead to the introduction of a **project** when the students will **make notes** about their involvement. A visit to the library where **research** skills would be implemented and then a return to the classroom for a further **discussion** on the information that has been collected and how it is to be presented.

COMBINING THEORY AND PRACTICE

Combining a variety of teaching methods enables theory and practice to be taught simultaneously. However, some teachers divorce theory from practice, and in some educational establishments they go as far as timetabling them separately. Often one session is timetabled for practical cookery and another one for theory, to include such topics as nutrition, food chemistry, dietetics, temperature, weights, measures and so on. These areas could just as easily be linked to the preparation and cooking of the food. Students would be able to see:

- the effects of different temperatures on the food they were preparing

- the way in which different starchy foods react when liquid is added

- the effects of different raising agents on a variety of mixtures.

They would also be able to calculate proportions and adapt quantities of ingredients, so that this aspect of mathematics is not taught in a sterile situation.

EXPERIMENTING IN THE CLASSROOM

Experimentation in teaching can add spark to the situation.
Make an effort to:

- keep up to date with your subject

- be enthusiastic

- employ innovative ideas.

In this way you will keep your lessons lively and fresh.

If you consider teaching to be a problem-solving activity then a certain amount of experimentation will be necessary to ensure success – for what works on one occasion may not work on another because each situation is affected by:

- the learning environment

- the existing knowledge of the students

- their motivation

- their needs

- their attitude to learning and so on.

It might be that your planned teaching methods need adapting or even abandoning altogether once you get into the classroom. With experience you will be able to experiment with a range of methods in order to use the best combination for a particular situation.

TEAM TEACHING

Because learning is becoming more student-centred and teachers are acting more as resource persons, teaching methods are changing. Teams of specialist staff are needed to:

- design new schemes of work which will provide the students with more involvement in their own learning

- provide tutorial and counselling support

- resource the lessons. Resource centres are needed with technicians to produce the resources and set up and service audio-visual equipment.

All this needs to be budgeted for by a team of staff with the necessary expertise.

Team teaching also refers to a group of teachers who are involved with the same students *eg* those following the same course such as nursery nursing or work preparation. The team of teachers have responsibility for planning, delivery, monitoring and assessing the course.

Choosing your method

This chapter has introduced you to a small selection of teaching methods, both learner- and teacher-centred. Their choice depends on a variety of factors and having made that choice different skills are needed by you and your students if they are to be put into practice successfully.

Using a combination of methods within the lesson will help prevent your students becoming bored.

CASE STUDIES

Sarah comes to the rescue

After Sarah's first week of observation Marion invited her to become involved in the students' practical session.

Because of Marion's competent demonstration the week before, everyone knew what they were supposed to be doing. However, it wasn't long before Sarah realised that *knowing* something didn't ensure they would be able to *apply* that knowledge.

'I tried making this pastry at home after Marion had demonstrated it last week but it didn't turn out like hers,' confided one of the students to Sarah. 'It was as heavy as lead,' she said.

'I'll watch you make it,' offered Sarah, 'to see if I can tell where you are going wrong.'

Sarah stopped the student as she was rubbing the fat into the flour. 'You need to handle it lightly,' she said. 'And lift your hands above the bowl to incorporate air.'

'Marion told us that last week and made it look so easy, but I don't seem to be doing it right,' said the student, looking despondent.

'Let me show you,' offered Sarah. 'Relax your fingers and rub your thumb against them lightly pressing the fat into the flour. Lift as you go – try to get a gentle rhythm going.'

The student followed Sarah's instructions and then welcomed her help as she rolled out the pastry. It turned out light and crisp and the student was delighted.

'You did a good job there,' said Marion. 'You produced a very satisfied customer.'

'And I got a real buzz out of seeing her achieve those skills,' said Sarah.

Sam considers appropriate teaching methods

Sam had made up his mind to put into practice what he had learned on his training course. He decided to demonstrate how to transplant seedlings and then let the students practise.

The students joined him in the greenhouse and he demonstrated the task. They then had a go with varying degrees of success. Some pots were overfilled with compost, some underfilled, some students didn't adequately cover the seedlings, some buried them completely, some underwatered, some washed the seedlings away. It was back to the drawing board for Sam.

He decided to use the, 'All do this with me now,' method.

'Put the compost into the pot until it comes up to that line below the rim,' he said, then waited until they all completed that part of the task.

He had to help one who lacked the hand and eye co-ordination to do this cleanly and he remembered what his tutor had said about having the physical ability to perform skills.

'Poke a hole in the centre of the compost with your dibber,' he went on and the students copied him.

'Now gently lift the seedling out of the tray and drop it into the hole...make sure the leaves are sticking out of the top of the hole before you firm the seedling in with your fingers like this.'

He carefully monitored their progress and then said, 'Now you do one on your own and I'll come round and help you.'

At the end of the lesson he said, 'Well done lads. You made a good job of that.' He smiled to himself and thought, I'm getting there at last.

Ray reluctantly seeks help

Ray did as his head of department had suggested and went to see the tutor with the engineering background. He explained the situation and said the poor test results were because his students hadn't read the notes he'd given them. He attempted to justify his teaching method by saying that that was how he had been taught.

'Initially we all teach in the way we were taught because we don't know any other,' said the tutor. 'That's why we need courses like this. I'm the tutor for the teaching methods section of the course which starts next week – I'm sure you'll find that useful.'

'In the meantime try out some of the methods described in the books on the reading list you were given before the start of the course.'

Ray looked blank.

'You have read the books on the reading list, haven't you?'

'Er...yes, yes.' Ray said. Then he hurried away to try to borrow them from the library.

POINTS FOR DISCUSSION

1. How would you explain to someone the difference between teacher-centred and learner-centred teaching methods?

2. Some teachers swear by the chalk and talk method of teaching. What arguments would you put forward in an attempt to persuade them to experiment with other methods?

3. How might you plan a lesson in your own subject to incorporate a variety of teaching methods?

6
Knowing Your Resources

WHAT ARE RESOURCES?

In chapter 5 we referred to a teaching method as the way in which the material to be learned is presented to the students, *eg* a lecture or a demonstration. These are all methods of communication and therefore need to make use of as many of the senses as possible.

During a lecture, students are likely to 'switch off' unless the lecturer has a dynamic method of delivery and keeps their interest by using appropriate resources (sometimes called teaching aids or learning aids) to illustrate the subject matter. These could be charts, maps, video recordings and so on. The lecture is the **method** of communication, the charts, maps, and video recordings are the **resources** used to aid the method. Guard against regarding equipment (hardware) as a resource or learning aid – software needs to be produced to convey the information. The only time the hardware becomes a learning aid is when it is being used as a model for learning how to use it.

Resources are sometimes referred to as 'visual aids' but senses other than sight need to be used. For example, when using the demonstration method of teaching the teacher may involve the students in touching, smelling and tasting as well as seeing and hearing.

WHAT IS THEIR PURPOSE?

The main purpose of a resource is to aid communication but it does have other functions too, such as:

- It captures the students' interest in the subject to be learned. This can be done by showing an example of a finished article before demonstrating how to make it. This would also indicate the standard of work required.

- It gets a response from the students. An appropriate resource can trigger their thinking (cognitive response) and feelings (affective response).

- It prevents boredom. An imaginative resource may be just what is needed to intrigue the students and enliven dull subject matter.

- It motivates the students. Resources used to simplify a skill often results in the students wanting to 'have a go'.

- It enables the teacher to cope with different levels of ability. Self-help resources such as workbooks and computer programs allow her to spend more time with individuals.

- It can assist in summarising at the end of a lesson. Stage specimens can be used for a quick re-run of a demonstration.

DO YOU NEED RESOURCES?

Resources need to be exactly right for their job and their job is to help the students to learn. They should not be used to impress the students or the teaching practice supervisor.

Many resources are expensive to produce in terms of time and money. Always consider whether they justify this expense. Ask yourself:

- Could the time taken to produce a particular teaching aid be more profitably used?

- Will I be able to use it on more than one occasion?

- Can I make it robust enough for the students to handle?

Of course there are many commercially produced resources that you could buy or borrow, such as films, video recordings, projector slides and so on, but often they are not quite right for the lesson that has been planned. If you teach in a college with a resource department the technicians may produce teaching aids to your specification. However, sometimes it is the simplest resource that is the most useful, such as Sam's cardboard cone. (See case study at the end of this chapter.)

Whenever possible the real thing is preferable to a model or

Information conveyed by resources

Audio	Visual	Audio–visual
Radio broadcasts	Books	Slide projector plus tape recorder
Tape recordings	Handouts	Films
Compact disks	Chalkboards	TV productions
Language labs	Dry/wet boards	Video recordings
	Flannel boards	Computers
	Magnetic boards	Teacher
	Wall charts	
	Models	
	Projector slides	
	OHP slides	
	Stage specimens	

OHP = Overhead projector

Fig. 10. Examples of audio and visual resources.

picture. For example, when teaching botany a growing plant will convey much more information than a picture which can't show its reaction when handled or exposed to certain conditions.

Resources should aid learning. If a resource is the best way of guiding your students from their present level of learning to a more complex one then use it but always remember that you, the teacher, are your own best resource.

Producing a handout with notes and diagrams of how to perform a yoga posture is useful to take away from the lesson as a reminder of the technique. It cannot, however, replace a demonstration by a competent teacher, who can point out how to avoid injury.

CONSIDERING THE RANGE

There is a wide variety of resources to choose from. They range from boards displaying information to sophisticated models or computers complete with compact disks.

Look back at the learning situations that you have been involved in and try to recall the resources used.

Figure 10 shows a range of audio and visual resources.

ARE THEY USEFUL?

Below are a few examples of resources indicating:

1. their usefulness as aids to learning

2. points you need to consider before choosing them.

Chalk and dry/wet wipe boards

Usefulness
• Little preparation is needed.

• Information can be developed as the lesson progresses.

• Alterations to information can easily be made.

• They can be wiped clean and re-used.

Considerations
• You need to be competent at writing and drawing on the board.

- Chalkboards can be messy.

- Thought must be given to the way the information is arranged on the board otherwise it may develop into a scribbling pad and so confuse your students.

- It is difficult to face your class when using the board.

Magnetic, felt and flannel boards

Usefulness
- They allow movement of the models and illustrations to show alternative arrangements *eg* room layouts, map routes, flower arrangements.

- Once prepared they can be used repeatedly.

- Magnetic models can be used on any magnetic surface *eg* a filing cabinet.

- A blanket thrown over a chair can be used if a flannel or felt board isn't available.

- They can be used by students as self-help equipment.

Considerations
- Suitable models and illustrations take time to prepare – they have to be backed with magnets or velcro – do you have the time?

- Do you have storage space for the boards?

Wall charts and maps

Usefulness
- You can produce them for a particular lesson with just the information that you need.

- Commercially produced ones can be obtained and these are usually robust and well presented.

- They can be used repeatedly.

• You can face the class when referring to them.

Considerations
• If too much information is displayed your students could become confused and switch off.

• Detailed charts and maps are time consuming to prepare – do you have the time?

• They need to be large unless you intend to use them for small group teaching.

• If left on the wall permanently they will lose their impact – do you have storage facilities?

Software for the overhead projector

Usefulness
• Transparencies can be prepared before the lesson.

• An overlay sequence can be produced so that notes and diagrams can be built up as the lesson progresses.

• They can be used repeatedly.

• Transparencies can be photocopied and issued as handouts.

• A roll of acetate can be clipped on to the projector and used instead of a board. It can be rolled backwards and forwards for recapping during the lesson and then removed for future use.

• You can face your students when using the projector.

Considerations
• You need to be able to draw and write legibly.

• An overlay sequence is time consuming to prepare and diagrams that are being built up using overlays must be 'spot on'.

• If you are using it instead of a chalkboard the same considerations apply.

Software for the slide projector

Usefulness
- You can produce your own slides so that they are appropriate for a particular lesson.

- They can be used repeatedly.

- The projector can be operated manually so that the pace of the lesson can be controlled.

- It can be operated with impulses from a tape recorder so allowing a synchronised audio–visual presentation.

- Commercially produced slides are available.

Considerations
- Are you competent enough to produce your own slides?

- Do you have the time to produce them?

- Commercially produced slides can be expensive – is money available?

- Are the commercially produced slides exactly right for your planned lesson?

- You need to make arrangements before the lesson for the projector to be available.

Films, television productions and video recordings

Usefulness
- Commercially produced programmes are usually of a higher quality than the ones a teacher can produce.

- Situations can be shown that the students may not otherwise have the chance of seeing, *eg* surgical operations or life in other countries.

- They are useful for pre- and post-programme discussions.

Considerations
- They can be expensive to hire – is money available?

- Is it possible for you to view the film or programme before showing it to the students? If not it may turn out to be unsuitable and so a waste of time.

- The timing of television productions may not coincide with the time of your lesson. Is recording equipment available?

- The length of the programme may not coincide with the length of your lesson.

- You will have handed over your class for the duration of the film or programme.

Computers

Usefulness
- The vast range of software available now makes the computer a valuable and sophisticated aid to learning.

- Disks can be tailor-made to specific student requirements.

- Students can interact with the information on the screen.

- It can provide the student with instant feedback.

Considerations
- You need to be computer literate.

- If your students haven't been brought up with computers they may lack the confidence to use them.

- They are expensive pieces of equipment – if they are not available for every student other activities need to be planned.

- The computer is only as good as the software produced.

- They do little to foster interaction between students.

RESOURCING YOUR METHODS

The selection of resources for a particular lesson will depend, to a certain extent, on:

1. Their appropriateness for the teaching method you have chosen and the ability of your students.

2. The equipment available to present the resource.

3. Your ability to use the equipment.

4. Your available time to produce them.

Below is a list of topics with suggested ways of resourcing the teaching methods.

TOPIC – Map reading

Teaching methods	Resources
Discussion of routes and symbols on poster.	*Large poster* of ordnance survey map of local area.
Question/answer session on symbols.	*Handout* of map symbols.
Students travel a given route inserting symbols on the map.	*Handout* of map.
Teacher and students check completed maps from transparencies on overhead projector.	*Flap sequence* of OHP transparencies.

TOPIC – The digestive tract

Teaching methods	Resources
Question/answer session on 'Where does food go once it has entered the mouth?'.	List of organs on *chalkboard*.
Groupwork – students to *discuss*, come to a consensus and *label a handout* with the organs of the digestive tract.	*Unlabelled* handout.

Teaching methods	Resources
Students indicate to teacher where to put labels on magnetic board.	*Magnetic board* displaying an unlabelled digestive tract.
Teacher corrects students' mistakes.	*Magnetic labels.*
Students handle life-size model of digestive tract – *naming* each part as they do so.	*Model* of digestive tract.

TOPIC – Spread of infection

Teaching methods	Resources
Students suggest ways in which infection can be spread.	
Teacher makes a chalkboard summary.	*Chalkboard.*
Students watch film on the spread of infection showing speed of bacteria multiplying.	*Film projector and film.*
Discussion of film. *Students make notes* on salient points.	

CASE STUDIES

Sarah considers her resources

'Would you like to give the demonstration next week?' Marion asked Sarah at the end of the cookery practical class.

'I'd love to – that's something I know I can do well,' said Sarah confidently.

'Well, don't forget the purpose of a demonstration is to show the students the skills involved in making the dish – not to flaunt your skills as a performer.' Marion hoped she hadn't sounded too pedantic.

'Yes, I realise that,' said Sarah. 'I found that out to my cost – I lost all my class. I'll try not to lose yours,' she said facetiously.

'Take next week's topic from my scheme of work,' said Marion, 'and plan the lesson. It follows on from what we've been doing this week.'

Sarah was already thinking how she would tackle the lesson as they went into the staff room for a cup of tea.

'I'll come in early next week and prepare the demonstration,' she said. 'And I'll write the recipe on the board so that the students can copy it while I'm demonstrating.'

'The problem with that method,' said Marion, 'is that while the students are copying from the board they aren't concentrating on your demonstration. It's difficult to do two things at once unless, of course, one is a habit.'

'Mm. I see what you mean,' said Sarah. 'Would it be better to let them copy the recipe after the demonstration?'

'Think about the time involved when you use note-taking as a method of providing your students with information. There's the time it takes you to put the notes on the board and the time it takes the students to copy them – some of the older ones are very slow at writing. Couldn't that time be more usefully used?'

'I suppose it could,' Sarah thought for a minute. 'I could put the recipe on a handout,' she said.

'That sounds a better idea,' said Marion. 'And the technician in the resource centre at college will run off some copies for you. Don't forget to sign them out to the adult education department – the cost will come out of our budget. Always keep a copy so that you can reproduce more when you demonstrate this dish again.'

Things were beginning to click into place for Sarah. She now knew that not only had the method of teaching to be considered, but resources had to be chosen that were appropriate for the method and the ability of the students.

Sam uses his imagination

Sam thought a lot about the ability of his students and wondered whether, by using teaching aids, he could help them master some of the gardening skills. He thought about the 'ruler' his colleague had made for measuring table legs and decided to adopt the idea for use in the vegetable garden. He made one ruler and tried it out in his own garden before asking the woodwork group to make one each for his students. The rulers were chunky pieces of wood, ten centimetres long and with an easy to grasp handle on the top.

'Right, lads,' he said one morning after they had prepared the soil, 'we are going to plant peas. They have to be planted ten centimetres apart. Who knows how far apart ten centimetres is?' No one responded.

'Well, to make it easy for you I've got rulers that are exactly the right length.' Sam gave out the rulers.

He demonstrated what he wanted them to do – to mark the soil at ten centimetre intervals and then make a hole with a dibber and drop in one pea seed.

The rulers were a success – the problem lay in getting one pea into the hole. Sometimes two or three were dropped into one hole, and occasionally the peas rolled away leaving some holes without a pea.

During break Sam produced triangles of card and took them with a stapling gun into the greenhouse. He showed the students how to fold the triangle and staple it to make a cone with a hole at the bottom.

'Come on lads – we'll plant another row of peas,' he said. They watched as Sam held the cone over the hole and dropped in one pea – they followed suit.

The simple resource worked.

Ray produces a useful resource

Ray read the books on teaching methods, which also suggested appropriate resources. He could see that many of them were time consuming to prepare and he wasn't convinced they were worth the trouble.

However, he thought he ought to make an effort as his head of department had already reminded him that he was still on probation. So he found a complex diagram in a book and copied it meticulously on to a large sheet of card so that he could pin it up on the wall for the students to copy.

The lesson was a flop. The students were totally confused by the large amount of information presented to them at one time.

'I spent hours producing that poster,' he told his tutor. 'And it was a waste of time.'

'What was the purpose of the poster?' asked the tutor.

'It was instead of putting the diagram on the board. I thought it would save time in the lesson but it didn't. Some of them didn't even finish it.'

'When you put diagrams on the board you build them up a little at a time – allowing the students to grasp the significance of one bit of detail before moving on to the next.'

'But the problem is,' said Ray, 'It has to be rubbed off at the end of the lesson. I thought by producing a poster I could use it over and over again.'

'Why don't you make a flap sequence of acetates for the overhead projector? You can then reveal one stage at a time as you would on the board – building up the competed diagram.'

'I'm not sure how to go about it,' said Ray.

'In exactly the same way as you would draw it on the board,' said the tutor. 'Draw the first stage of the diagram on the bottom acetate, the second stage on the second acetate and so on, until you've built up the completed diagram. Make sure all the stages overlay each other exactly before fastening them together. If you go into the resource centre the technician will give you a hand – he'll provide you with the acetates and the appropriate coloured pens too.'

Ray was pleased with the result and it did save time in the lesson. Instead of drawing on the board he was able to go around the class and monitor the students as they produced the diagram. He could also take the resource away with him to use on other occasions – which appealed to Ray.

POINTS FOR DISCUSSION

1. How might resources change the way you teach your subject?

2. Do you think resources will eventually make teachers redundant?

3. How would you justify your use of resources to someone who considers them a waste of time?

7
Assessing Learning

WHY ASSESS?

Assessment should be an ongoing process, taking place:

- before the new learning is introduced, to assess whether your students have the necessary skills to build on

- throughout the new learning, to enable you to diagnose any learning difficulties your students may be having

- at the end of the learning period to assess achievement.

If your students fail to achieve the new learning an assessment will need to be made of your teaching.

CHOOSING AN ASSESSMENT METHOD

Your choice of assessment method will depend on several factors.

1. The type of **learning** to be assessed. Is it:
   (a) cognitive (thinking) learning
   (b) motor learning (physical)
   or are you making judgements about your students' attitudes, enthusiasm, motivation and so on?

2. The **ability** of your students. It would be useless trying to test their knowledge of safety procedures in the workshop by giving them a written test if they couldn't write.

3. The **facilities** available. Do you have sufficient pieces of equipment for every student to be tested at the same time? A verbal explanation of how to use equipment can only test knowledge, not practical ability.

What assessment methods have you experienced? Do you know what type of learning they were testing? Below is a selection of testing methods that can be used to assess a variety of skills.

Testing method	Used to test
essay multiple choice question and answer discussion project	cognitive skills
oral test	languages
aural test	musical ability
practical test	(a) motor skills *eg* ability to manipulate equipment (b) cognitive skills *eg* an understanding of the purpose and sequence of operations (c) originality, innovation, persistence and so on.

ASSESSING MOTOR (PHYSICAL) SKILLS

If you teach a practical subject then you will always be observing your students' motor-skills performance. Occasionally you may have to assess them formally unless of course yours is a recreational class – then it would not be advisable. It would be a sure way to empty your class.

However, you will be able to observe them working and judge their skills from week to week – guiding and correcting whenever necessary.

For those of you who have to mark a practical test under examination conditions the following information may be useful.

Marking a practical test

The most important thing when marking any type of test is not to let your own views and feelings influence your judgement. This is known as **subjectivity** and must be avoided at all costs for you need to be accountable to your students. You must stick rigidly to the marking scheme.

If you have to produce your own marking scheme you need to:

• state clearly what your students must do to gain the marks

• allocate marks for each section of the test.

Consider the following two marking schemes:

1. The students will prepare and paint a door   20 marks

2. The students will:
   (a) gather together – sandpaper   1 mark
                        – damp cloth   1 mark
                        – paint   1 mark
                        – brush   1 mark
                        – turps   1 mark
   (b) sand down the door until it is smooth   3 marks
   (c) remove all dust with damp cloth   1 mark
   (d) load brush with paint   2 marks
   (e) apply paint to door – long even strokes   4 marks
   (f) check for runs – brush them away   3 marks
   (g) wipe up any drips immediately   2 marks
                                              total   20 marks

Using scheme two will enable you to be accountable to your students. When one of them asks why he only got 11 out of 20 when his neighbour got 13, you will be able to tell him!

An experienced teacher can tell by observation which is the more skilled student but he needs to be able to provide each one with detailed feedback about his performance. If every element of the task is performed correctly then the product will be perfect.

Providing feedback in stages
In some cases it is important for the examiner to point out mistakes before allowing the student to carry on, otherwise a mistake made in the initial stages of a test may affect all subsequent stages. For example, if the dressmaking student lays the pattern on the fabric incorrectly and then is allowed to cut it out, the dress may end up with two left sleeves or only one half of the skirt. By getting the student to correct the 'lay' the examiner will ensure the student has a fair chance of showing her skill in the other stages of the test – of course marks for the 'lay' are lost.

Similarly if a student adds too much liquid to the pastry in a cookery test so that it is too wet to handle she will be unable to show her skill at the rolling out stage. The examiner needs to allow her to remake the pastry so that she is able to demonstrate the other skills needed to complete the pie.

Show your students the marking scheme
It is important that your students are made aware of the marking scheme well in advance of the test. They need to know that every skill is tested separately so that a student who drops her pie as she is taking it out of the oven doesn't go to pieces thinking she has failed the test completely. She will know that she has only lost the marks for presentation.

When producing your marking scheme keep the numbers small for each element of the task so that you don't let your own feelings influence your judgement. Imagine having to justify giving one student 38 out of 50 and another one only 36!

Marking out of 3 is useful. The skill is either perfect and receives 3 marks, or is acceptable and receives 2 marks or is in need of improvement and receives 1 mark.

ASSESSING COGNITIVE (THINKING) SKILLS

It is just as important to stick to the marking scheme when marking cognitive skills as motor skills.

When assessing an essay you might be inclined to give a few extra marks to the student who is a neat writer because it makes it easier for you to read. But are you supposed to be assessing neatness of writing? If so it should be on your marking scheme and your students should be told.

Tell your students what you will be looking for and how you will allocate the marks. For example:

Assessing an essay

	Marks
A clear introduction to the topic outlining how the essay will be developed	3
Developing the essay as outlined	3
Producing logical arguments	4
Summarising main points	3
Neatness of presentation	2
	15

It is interesting to put a group of students together and ask them to produce a marking scheme for a particular examination question. They will argue about the importance of each element of the question and the number of marks to be allocated.

Incidentally, an exercise like this will benefit your students when they take a written examination, as it will draw their attention to the salient parts of each question.

PRODUCING AN ASSESSMENT SCHEDULE

Before producing a detailed marking scheme you should look closely at the task to be assessed, consider the types of skills involved and the relative importance of each skill. This information can be displayed on an **assessment schedule**. You can then decide how to allocate the marks.

Example: photography
Consider a subject like photography which involves:

- an understanding of the camera's capabilities

- an ability to judge which subject to take

- skill in taking the photograph

- enthusiasm

- patience

- artistic flair.

Here you can see that motor and cognitive skills are involved as well as attitudes and a degree of invention.

1. The **motor skills** of taking the photographs.

2. The **cognitive skills** involved in:
    (a) understanding how the camera works
    (b) making judgements about where and when to take the photographs
    (c) applying knowledge and understanding to taking the photographs.

skills	motor	cognitive	invention	attitude	totals
understanding the camera's capabilities		8			8
judging which subject to take		4	2		6
taking the photograph	2	6			8
enthusiasm				2	2
patience				2	2
artistic flair			4		4
					Total 30

Fig. 11. An example of a photography assessment schedule.

3. **Attitudes** and **invention** displayed in:
   (a) the curiosity and enthusiasm to seek out subjects to photograph
   (b) the patience to wait for hours in appalling weather to get just the right photograph
   (c) a feeling for what will make a perfect picture.

Bearing this information in mind the assessment schedule might look something like the one in Figure 11.

Teachers with an in-depth knowledge of photography will probably want to argue with the number of marks allocated to each section of the assessment schedule. Some might consider that more marks should be given for taking the photograph, whereas others might want extra marks for artistic flair. So you see even with an objective assessment schedule subjectivity can creep in at the production stage.

It is inevitable that value judgements will be made, for we all attach more importance to some things than others. Take, for example, the skating skills of Torvill and Dean – their mechanical skills can be quantified, but their artistic flair which produces the magical performance is a difficult phenomenon to assess. We *feel* its perfection.

Once the schedule has been completed a marking scheme can be produced and the marks for each area of the schedule allocated when the test is produced.

Producing the tests

The choice of tests will depend on the skills you are testing. A practical test would be the obvious choice for the above assessment schedule but it would be possible to test the students' understanding of the camera's capabilities in a written test.

When devising the tests the assessor needs to ask, 'What do the students have to do to indicate that they:

- understand the camera's capabilities

- can judge which subject to take

- can take the photograph

- are enthusiastic

- have patience

- have artistic flair?'

Assessment schedule for a Basic Social Care course

subject	knowledge	understanding	application	motor skills	attitude	innovation	totals
Human growth and development							
Social studies							
First aid							
Environmental studies							
Home economics							
Crafts							
Total $\longrightarrow$							

Fig. 12. An example of an assessment schedule for a course.

Appropriate tests must then be produced – ones that will enable the students to indicate their skill in all areas.

Assessment of courses

Assessment schedules can be produced for a whole course as well as for a single topic (see Figure 12). This is an assessment schedule for a basic Social Care course.

As well as testing in these subject areas a profile of each student would be produced in order to assess whether he or she was a suitable candidate for the caring professions. A student may receive high marks in the subjects on the assessment schedule but be inadequate when it comes to relating to people.

PROFILING

Creating a comprehensive record

Profiling is a way of recording the capabilities of the 'whole' student, not just her thinking and practical abilities but her:

- manner and attitude towards her peers, those in authority and the people with whom she comes into contact

- ability to take responsibility

- skill in decision-making

- general appearance

- ability to communicate effectively

- punctuality, and so on.

Completing profiles

A profile record is completed by:

- members of the teaching staff

- staff in work experience establishments

- the student herself.

One of the main criticisms of profiling is that it is time consuming. In order to produce an informative profile each student needs to be reviewed regularly and a progress report made which leads to the final profile – all of which takes time.

Involving the students

Students are involved at each stage of profiling. This is an improvement on traditional methods when students weren't allowed to see the marking scheme or told how the assessor had arrived at the result. However, when students are asked by the teacher how they rate their own performance some undervalue or overvalue themselves. This then requires a specially trained teacher to spend time helping them to make a more realistic assessment of themselves.

Some staff in work experience establishments occasionally complain that they haven't the time or the necessary skills to assess students and some don't see it as their job anyway. On the other hand, many are glad to give their time and will readily discuss a student's progress with her tutor.

A well produced profile:

• gives an informed view of a student's abilities both academic and social

• does not rely on one teacher's assessment of a student

• is ongoing so that the student is receiving feedback along the way

• encourages the student to make judgements about her own performance.

The criticisms of profiling seem to be ones of management and organisation rather than means of assessment.

CASE STUDIES

Sarah makes some assessments without a test

Sarah knew Marion's students quite well which helped to dispel some of her nervousness when she took over the class. She gave out copies of the recipe before her demonstration and discussed it with the students, clearing up any misconceptions they had about the ingredients and method.

Before starting to demonstrate she drew their attention to the pictures she had pinned on the display board. They showed a variety of dishes that could be made from the basic recipe. Also she had brought in a selection of recipe books for them to browse through while her dishes were cooking – these provided material for discussion.

The lesson was a success.

'Well done,' said Marion after the students had left. 'I particularly liked your resources. The pictures helped them to see that once they'd mastered the basic skill they could experiment and adapt it to produce more elaborate dishes.'

'Yes,' said Sarah. 'I listened to their comments. Some were enthusiastic and quite knowledgeable about how to set about adapting the recipe – others for one reason or another said they would stick to the basic recipe.'

'Some of them aren't very adventurous,' said Marion, 'and some, of course, can't afford to make more elaborate dishes. By observing and listening you learn a lot about your students. As you say it gave you some idea of their existing knowledge and also their enthusiasm. But it won't be possible for you to assess their practical skills in producing the dish that you demonstrated until you observe them making it next week.'

Sam profiles his students

'We're producing a profile on each of your students,' the head of department told Sam. I want you to complete it at the end of each month.'

Sam panicked. 'A what?'

'It's an ongoing report on each of the students – recording their progress.'

'What do I have to do? I've no experience of writing reports – I work with my hands not a pen.'

'Stop panicking,' said the head. 'I've watched you with the students. You're doing a good job. The form is already printed out so all you need to do is tick one of the boxes at the side of each skill to indicate whether the student is competent or needs more help.'

The head showed Sam the form with the list of skills down the left-hand side, the tick boxes in the middle and a section on the right for 'further comments'.

Sam looked at the skills which included things like, attendance, punctuality, ability to work with others, manual dexterity and so on.

'What sort of things do I put in this column that says "further comments"?' asked Sam.

'Anything you've particularly noticed about a student. For example his manual dexterity may have improved considerably even though he still needs more help. The profile allows you to make a comment about such things.'

After completing the first month's profiles Sam found himself watching the students carefully and making mental notes of any changes in their performances so that he could give a more rounded assessment of their capabilities when he completed the profiles.

Ray is given food for thought

Ray discussed his lesson with a senior tutor in engineering.

'Some of the lads are pretty good at drawing,' he said – 'almost like photographic copies. Others haven't a clue. They don't seem to be able to see the relationship of one part to another.'

'Do they know the relationship?' asked the tutor.

'That's what I'm going to do after break,' said Ray. 'I'm going to deal with each part of the diagram and show its relationship to the whole. Initially I just wanted to be able to assess their ability to copy the diagram '

'I'm glad you realise that that is all you would be able to do. Copying is pretty low-level stuff. Would it not have been better to reverse your method – ensure they understood first and then assessed whether they could apply that understanding?'

Ray wasn't sure. 'I wanted to use this visual aid I've produced,' he said, taking the flap sequence of acetates out of his folder and showing the tutor. 'What do you think?'

'Mm. It's an excellent teaching aid is this – well made too. Use it to build up their understanding of the topic in small stages. Then set them some test exercises to assess their ability to apply that understanding.'

'But they wouldn't have a diagram,' said Ray.

'Photocopy your final acetate and give them a copy, unless you want to assess their skill in drawing – if so build it into your test exercises.'

Ray went away to think about these suggestions.

POINTS FOR DISCUSSION

1. From the wide variety of assessment techniques available what would influence your choice?

2. Of what use is a knowledge of the levels of learning to a teacher who is preparing a marking scheme?

3. How would you explain to somebody the meaning of the term 'profiling'?

8
How to Plan Your Lesson

THINKING ABOUT YOUR PLAN

Before you start to plan your lesson the following questions need to be asked:

- What am I going to teach?
- What do I know about my students?
- What skills do I want my students to learn?

What am I going to teach?

The topic for a particular lesson will show up on your scheme of work which you will have produced at the beginning of the course. (If you teach an examination subject your scheme of work will have been produced from the examining board's syllabus – probably by the course organiser.) The topics will follow a logical sequence so that your students learn the simpler skills at the beginning of the course before moving on to the more complex.

What do I know about my students?

If the lesson that you are about to plan is the first on your scheme of work you may not have met your students. If this is the case then your plan needs to be flexible and you must be prepared to adapt it during the lesson if necessary. If, on the other hand, you are several weeks into the course you will have got to know your students and their capabilities. You will probably also be aware of their interests and should take these into consideration at the planning stage of the lesson.

For example, a student may be skilled in a field that is relevant to your subject. She may be a specialist in aromatherapy and be prepared to discuss it with your yoga students or she may cultivate herbs and be glad to share her knowledge with your cookery students. Allocate time for this in your lesson plan.

What skills do I want my students to learn?

These skills will obviously depend on the topic and the tasks involved. Your ability to break down each task into its component parts will help you identify the skills you want your students to learn.

Perhaps you teach sports such as cricket, rugby, football or golf. Many of the tasks contained in these sports are physical, such as throwing, catching, kicking, batting and so on. You need to be able to analyse them to identify the motor skills involved.

Skills involved in cricket

The batsman in cricket needs to be able to:

- stand correctly
- grasp the bat
- swing his arms and so on.

Combined with these motor skills are cognitive (thinking) skills such as making judgements about:

- the type of ball being delivered
- how to strike it
- where to position it on the field.

And while all this is going on the batsman may be displaying his apprehension, fear, confidence, enjoyment (affective states). Confidence and enjoyment will come as he masters the skills that you are planning to teach.

Some of you may teach subjects that only involve cognitive skills and so will require a lesson plan that takes this into consideration.

Learning about astronomy

If your subject is astronomy you will want your students to learn about planets. You could plan to tell them that:

- there are nine planets
- they revolve in elliptical orbits around the sun
- there are also other bodies, called comets, that revolve around the sun.

These facts could all be learned parrot fashion.

However, you may then want to go on to teach them to discriminate between planets and comets which is a more complex skill and will require you to plan different teaching methods.

CHOOSING YOUR TEACHING METHOD

Having considered the skills that you want your students to learn you need to choose an appropriate teaching method. We dealt with a variety of these in chapter 5.

Methods for practical subjects

Those of you who teach practical subjects will obviously need to include a demonstration in your lesson, followed as soon as possible by your students' practice. You may also want to allow time for discussions and note-making.

Methods for cognitive subjects

A variety of activities helps to avoid the students becoming bored and this needs to be taken into account, particularly when teaching cognitive (thinking) skills. It is a good idea to intersperse lectures, discussions and note-making with group work, or the showing of slides or video-recordings if they are appropriate.

The methods you plan should be the best ones for the job. Science and engineering subjects will come alive with industrial visits so whenever possible try to organise these. Often firms have specially trained staff to conduct the visits. This ensures that your students are kept up to date with the latest technology.

ALLOCATING TIME

Lessons may be as short as 45 minutes or as long as three hours and it is only with experience that you will be able to judge how much you can fit into a given length of time. The important thing to remember is that if your students haven't grasped the learning in the lesson it is useless going on to the next stage as they will have nothing to build on. The lesson will have to be replanned and repeated, otherwise subsequent teaching will be a waste of time. If it is just an isolated student who is floundering then perhaps a private session with follow-up homework will solve the problem.

It is important to bear in mind also that if time is running out it is much better to wind up the lesson at a convenient place rather than rushing to cram in the content of the lesson plan.

Planning the timing

The timing on a lesson plan can only ever be a guide as there are so many unforeseen events that may crop up in the lesson. Putting actual times on your plan can be useful so that:

1. You know when to stop one activity and start another. If you allow 20 minutes for a discussion you need to watch the time carefully. It could quite easily stretch to 40 minutes, leaving insufficient time for the next activity.

2. You avoid chaos. An art teacher who hasn't allowed time at the end of the lesson for the students to clear away their work or a cookery teacher with half-cooked pies still in the oven won't be very popular with the incoming teacher.

3. You allow sufficient time for your students to complete a task. You will very quickly learn that what takes you half an hour to demonstrate may take your students one and a half hours to practise.

CHOOSING RESOURCES

As pointed out in chapter 6 the choice of resources will depend on their suitability for the teaching methods being used. It will also depend on the amount of time you have available for their production. If time is at a premium you could adapt commercially produced ones.

Having made your choice you need to ensure that:

- The resource will be available when you need it – particularly if it is a film or a video-recording.

- The projector or video-recorder will be available.

- The room is appropriate for the resource *eg* that it has power points and tables and desks that can be moved to a position where all the students can see.

- When taking your students on a visit you have made all the necessary arrangements well in advance of the day and booked the transport.

CONSIDERING ASSESSMENT

Although you will be observing your students throughout the lesson in order to assess their progress and diagnose any learning difficulties it may be necessary also to plan a more formal type of assessment.

Planning for formal assessment

If you are preparing your students for an examination then you will need to provide them with practice in the type of procedures they are likely to meet.

They may be:

- multiple-choice questions
- essays
- oral tests
- practical tests
- short answer tests.

Whatever the type, practice time must be allowed for on your lesson plan.

Homework

The setting of homework consolidates what your students have learned in the classroom and this also needs to be considered at the planning stage of your lesson. Returning it and discussing it with individual students takes time. If it has to be done within the lesson then you will need to plan tasks to keep the remainder of the class occupied. Homework will also help you to assess whether your students are ready to move on to the next stage of learning.

Profiling

Just as the discussion of homework needs to be carried out on an individual basis so does profiling. A timetable needs to be produced and adhered to rigidly if every student is to be seen within the time limit.

PRODUCING YOUR LESSON PLAN

During the early stages of your teaching you will probably need to experiment with your lesson plan layouts and they are sure to be very detailed. As you gain confidence, however, you will find that headings and reminders are enough to make you feel comfortable in the classroom.

Too much detail is difficult to cope with and if you are always stopping to read copious notes you will lose your credibility with the students. Try to keep it simple.

Guide for lesson planning

It is a good idea to have a blank format to complete when planning your lessons such as that in Figure 13. It forces you to look at:

- timing
- what you will be doing
- what your students will be doing
- what resources you will need
- how you will assess learning.

Example of a lesson plan

Figure 14 shows the type of lesson plan that Sarah (case study) might have produced when she took over Marion's class for the cookery demonstration.

With more experience Sarah could produce something as simple as the following:

1.00	Discuss pictures Explain recipe
1.15	Demonstrate
2.00	Dish in oven – discuss recipes in books
2.30	Dish cooked – display – recap – and discuss
2.45	Clear room
3.00	End of lesson
Comments	

Comments

It is always a good idea to have a space on your lesson plan for comments. You can then make notes at the end of the lesson about things that have gone particularly well and are worth repeating or

Time	Teaching method	Students' activity	Resources	Assessment	Comments

Fig. 13. A blank format – a guide for lesson planning.

Cookery Demonstration – apple pie   (duration 2 hours)

12.45   Prepare room, collect ingredients, pin pictures on board, put out recipe books and recipe handouts.

1.00   Light oven. Welcome students. Recap on Marion's last lesson. Link it to today's lesson. Discuss pictures of dishes made from shortcrust pastry. Observe students' interest. Answer any questions.

1.10   Give out recipe sheets. Discuss ingredients and method. Clear up any misunderstandings.

1.15   Demonstrate with explanation how to make pastry. Prepare apples (suggest alternatives). Make pie. Answer any questions.

2.00   Put pie in oven. Recap on procedure and answer any questions. Encourage students to browse through cookery books for alternative dishes to make from shortcrust pastry.

2.30   Take pie from oven. Question students on their understanding of pastry making and pitfalls to avoid. Discuss next week's practical session.

2.45   Clear room.

3.00   Class finishes.

Fig. 14. An example of a lesson plan for a cookery demonstration.

things that need attention the next time you give the lesson. Perhaps the resources were confusing or the timing needs adjusting.

A columnar type of lesson plan is popular because it is easy to follow in the lesson. However, the headings may vary according to what you wish to remind yourself of. Some teachers have a column for board work. The advantage of this is that it forces them to pre-plan the board layout – but it can result in a very lengthy lesson plan.

An essay-type plan can be difficult to follow during a lesson if it is very lengthy but it can be simplified by highlighting the key instructions.

Whichever method you choose make sure that it follows a logical sequence and allow time for the completion of each stage.

Example of a logical sequence

Stage 1   Briefly remind your students of the previous lesson and check that they are ready to move on to the next stage of learning.

Stage 2   Introduce the new learning explaining how it links to what they already know. Indicate what you expect them to achieve.

Stage 3   Explain the format the lesson will take.

Stage 4   Carry out the planned teaching and guide your students through the planned learning – monitoring their progress.

Stage 5   Summarise and sort out any problems.

Stage 6   Allocate homework.

CASE STUDIES

Marion reassures Sarah

'You coped well with the practical class,' Marion told Sarah at the end of the lesson.

'So, how do you feel about having your tutor in to observe you next week?'

'Nervous,' said Sarah. 'I have to let her have a lesson plan a few days before the visit so that she can see what I'm going to be doing.'

'Well that's no problem, is it?' asked Marion. 'You've planned the last couple of lessons quite well.'

'I keep thinking of all the things that could go wrong.'

'Think positively,' said Marion. 'As long as you are well prepared you won't have any problems. Remember she isn't coming to catch you out, she's coming to see whether you are putting into practice the things you're learning on your training course and whether you need any help.'

'I've got a fairly straightforward outline of a plan that I'm going to use,' Sarah told Marion. 'It forces me to look at the timing for all the activities – mine and the students. At the side of each activity I have a space for resources and one for assessment even though most of the assessing will be done by observing or listening.'

'Are you going to use resources?' asked Marion.

'My husband has taken some slides of simple cake decorations so I'm going to show those after my demonstration – while my cake is in the oven.'

'That should interest them.'

'I've already booked the projector and screen.'

'Good. You seem to know what lesson planning is all about,' said Marion. 'You'll be fine, I'm sure.'

Sam plans to take his students on a visit

'Will it be all right if I take my students on a visit next week?' Sam asked his head of department.

'It'll depend on the staff situation. You can't take them on your own. Where were you thinking of going?'

'A garden centre that's just opened. It's only about five miles away.'

'Even so you'll need the minibus. Leave it with me and I'll let you know tomorrow.'

The following day the head sent for Sam.

'About this visit – make it Friday because Jane, the student on teaching practice, will be in, so she can go with you and Alf can drive the minibus. Let me have details of your plan for the day.'

Sam planned the visit to the last detail. He produced letters for the students' parents telling them where they were going and the time they would be back and asking them to provide packed lunches.

He was taking six students with learning difficulties. Three of them couldn't read so he paired them with the three who could.

On the Thursday before the visit Sam showed the head his plan.

'I've produced three booklets – one for each couple,' he said.

'I want to encourage their sight vocabulary so on one page I've listed words like entrance, exit, gents, ladies, and on each of the other pages I've written the name of a plant with a picture. I'll see how many they recognise. I've rung the garden centre and told them we're coming and they've promised that someone will be available to show us round.'

'Good,' said the head. 'You seem to have thought of everything. Enjoy yourselves.'

Ray is about to change his method of teaching

'You look as though you've got all the world's worries on your shoulders,' Ray's colleague said as he sat next to him in the staff room.

'I have,' said Ray. 'Listen to this. This is my next assignment on the training course. *Set up the conditions in your classroom for student-centred learning.*'

'So what's the problem? You just put the onus on your students to be responsible for their own learning. You do all the planning and organising and then act as a manager and a resource person in the classroom.'

'I'm not sure that I'm keen on that idea,' said Ray. 'It gives them the opportunity to get out of hand – then I might not be able to control them.'

'Well, you won't know if you don't give it a try, will you? I'm sure you'd enjoy your teaching more if you'd just relax – let go of your students. Tell you what,' suggested Ray's colleague, 'plan your lesson and let me have a look at it. We can iron out any snags before you get into the classroom.'

So Ray planned the lesson and the two of them sat down to discuss it.

'I'm not sure how much time to allow them to work on their own,' said Ray.

'You're still worried about not having control, aren't you? They won't be working on their own, you'll be monitoring, giving advice and assessing what they're doing. You'll be in control all the time but you'll be giving them the opportunity to produce ideas, put them into practice and see whether they work. I'm sure you'll enjoy it.'

'I'll let you know how I get on,' said Ray.

'You should be all right,' said his colleague. 'You've planned the lesson well.'

POINTS FOR DISCUSSION

1. Some teachers always teach 'off the tops of their heads'. What are the advantages of having a lesson plan?

2. When staff are absent you may have to take over someone else's lesson at the drop of a hat. What might be the difficulties of trying to teach a lesson from someone else's lesson plan?

3. What factors might cause you to change your lesson plan in the classroom?

9
Succeeding in the Classroom

OVERCOMING NERVES

Being a teacher in many ways is like being an actor, because:

- they both suffer from first night nerves

- the nerves disappear once they have got to know their audience

- they both start to enjoy what they are doing as soon as the audience indicate that they have accepted them. (This usually happens when they give the audience what they want.)

Actors have many ploys for dealing with first night nerves such as relaxation exercises, deep breathing techniques and so on. However, one of the most important factors in combatting nerves is knowing that you are well prepared. An actor who is unsure of his lines is bound to feel nervous, just as a teacher who hasn't prepared her lesson or is unsure of her subject will dread going into the classroom. She knows these shortcomings will quickly become apparent to her students.

BEING PREPARED

Knowing that your lesson is well prepared will give you confidence. So will knowing that you look your best. First impressions matter. Looking smart and professional and being a well prepared, confident teacher will go a long way to dispelling your nervousness and ensuring that your students respond well to you.

ORGANISING THE VENUE

Before your students arrive you need time in the classroom to prepare for the lesson. This isn't always possible if another class is in residence. However, if you have thought about the preparation of the room at the planning stage of your lesson you should be able to organise it fairly quickly. If you know your students well they will probably help with such things as:

- arranging the furniture appropriately

- pinning up posters

- getting out equipment

- cleaning the board if the previous teacher has failed to do so – information not related to your lesson can be distracting.

MEETING YOUR STUDENTS

Your first meeting with a new group of students sets the scene for the whole course, so it is important to get off to a good start. Remember that teaching is a two-way method of communicating. It is not just about transmitting information but about receiving messages as well. So while you are receiving messages from your students about their nervousness or enthusiasm they will be receiving messages from you about:

- the role you intend to adopt

- what you expect of them

- your interest in your subject

- your enthusiasm for teaching, and so on.

First impressions

It isn't only what you say but how you say it. Your manner and tone of voice indicate whether you have a genuine interest in satisfying your students' needs. At your first meeting they will be forming their impression of you, so:

- smile when you greet them

- have a positive manner

- indicate that you are in control

- tell them the form the lesson will take

- explain what you expect of them

- sort out any problems that may be worrying them

- reassure them.

GETTING STARTED

Always start on time. If you don't your students will stop arriving on time. Students attending recreational classes may have problems with transport or baby-sitters. Don't ignore them when they arrive late as Sarah did in the case study. Welcome them and if they have missed something important arrange to bring them up to date later – don't subject the whole class to a repeat of what has already been completed.

Students attending an examination course or a day-release course from industry need to arrive on time. This is part of their training and will be entered on their profile. Continual lateness needs to be sorted out early!

Forming groups

As you start the lesson make a mental note of where the students sit. Are they in groups – perhaps they already know one another – or are they sitting in isolation? Note whether the seating pattern changes – perhaps after break when they have shared a cup of tea.

Groups formed in the early stages of a course may stay together because the members feel secure. But try to prevent them from becoming too well established otherwise you might find hostility developing between groups. Your lesson planning can ensure that students move around, work individually, as a class, or in different groups.

Having welcomed your students it is time for you to put your lesson plan into practice and manage the classroom situation.

MANAGING YOUR CLASS

Managing the class is an important role of the teacher and a good manager creates a good working environment where the members know exactly what they are supposed to be doing and where it is leading them. In order to achieve this you need to:

- present your students with the learning objectives at the beginning of the lesson so they know exactly what they are supposed to achieve

- encourage them to make decisions about their learning

- guide and support your students

- indicate that their contributions are worthwhile

- motivate them along the way

- praise their achievements.

HOW IS IT GOING?

During the lesson it is important that you monitor the situation carefully. Ask yourself the following questions:

1. Have the students understood my initial instructions?

2. Are they coping? If not why not?

3. Do I need to re-demonstrate – to an individual student or the whole group?

4. Am I on time? If not can I get back on time or shall I reschedule my lesson plan?

5. What can I leave out?

6. Am I going to have time to assess learning?

These and many other questions need to be at the forefront of your mind throughout the lesson – needless to say with experience it becomes an automatic process.

PROMPTING YOUR STUDENTS

Some of your time in the classroom will be spent prompting your students to ensure that learning progresses.

When learning a practical task once they have mastered the skills they need to string them together and it is at this stage that you may need to prompt.

Prompting is often used by driving instructors. For example once the learner can:

- switch on the engine
- engage the gear
- check mirrors
- pull away smoothly
- and negotiate traffic

he then needs to be able to string these skills together to perform the task of driving the car.

In the initial stages the instructor is on hand to aid the memory by saying 'mirror', 'change down', 'signal' and so on. Eventually this prompting can be faded out as the learner becomes more proficient. Each subordinate skill becomes the cue for the next one, just as the last words of a speech in a play serve as a cue for another actor to enter or speak.

It is often useful to ask your students to say out loud the actions they are performing as each action will trigger off the next one. Once they can do this without you prompting it will fade into internal speech and eventually into thought. So the skills become habit.

PROVIDING FEEDBACK

As your students perform the skills, be they cognitive or motor, they will look to you for feedback about their progress. The way in which you provide that feedback is most important – a friendly reassuring manner is what is needed.

Often the student knows there is a problem by the result of the learning activity itself. For example, if a message appears on the computer screen telling her that there is a 'data error' she knows she hasn't been successful in mastering the task. If when learning to ride a bicycle she is continually falling off she knows she must keep practising to achieve balance.

Try to pinpoint exactly where the problem lies – particularly in cognitive learning – and re-teach that element only, setting the student back on the right thinking track. Don't solve the whole problem for him but guide him towards solving it for himself.

Personal success is a vital motivator and is what you should be leading your students towards.

CHECKLIST

Once you set foot in the classroom the stage is yours and you can give either a good or a poor performance. The performance is measured by the way you set up the conditions and guide your students towards achieving the learning goals. Check that you have carried out the following tasks to the best of your ability:

- Planned the lesson with consideration for your students, your subject and the resources available.

- Prepared your room appropriately.

- Put your students at ease by adopting a friendly approachable manner.

- Created a good learning environment, by managing the class so that they gel as a group and support one another in their learning.

- Monitored the students' progress and provided them with appropriate feedback.

CASE STUDIES

Sarah's supervisor observes her lesson

Sarah arrived in the classroom early on the day she was being observed by her supervisor. She cleaned the chalkboard, set up the slide projector, prepared her demonstration and ensured that everything was ready for the lesson.

Her supervisor arrived early. 'You seem to be well prepared, Sarah,' she said. 'I've looked through your lesson plan and it's obvious you have put a great deal of thought into it.'

The students started to arrive and made their way to the chairs that Sarah had positioned around the demonstration table.

'I'll sit at the end here,' whispered the supervisor. 'Try to relax and ignore me. I'm not here to criticise. To be quite honest I'm looking forward to having an expert show me how to make a perfect sponge cake. Mine always sink in the middle!'

Sarah started the lesson by introducing her supervisor, saying that she was not a new student but that she was there to observe her teach. One or two of the students looked nervous. 'You can all relax,' she went on, 'she won't be asking you any awkward questions because she has just told me that her sponge cakes always sink in the middle so she will be concentrating on the demonstration.'

The students laughingly made light-hearted comments about the problem they had with their own sponge cakes.

While Sarah's cake was in the oven she showed them the slides of simple cake decorations. One of the slides had been put in the carousel upside down. 'Oops!' said Sarah, a little unnerved. 'Perhaps you'd like to stand on your heads for this one.'

Each slide prompted a great deal of discussion and there were times when Sarah found it difficult to make herself heard above the buzz of conversation. One of the students came to her rescue by reminding her that it was time to take the cake out of the oven – this changed the focus of their attention.

Because time was running out the summary of the lesson had to be cut short. There was only just time to organise the students for their practical session the following week.

Before the supervisor left she asked Sarah to produce her own evaluation of the lesson before she discussed it with her during the arranged tutorial.

The visit gives Sam food for thought

Sam and Jane, the student teacher, met the students in the front hall of the college. 'All got your packed lunches?' Sam asked. Everyone nodded. 'Right. Now get into your pairs that we agreed yesterday.' The students found their partners and Sam gave each pair a booklet that he'd prepared. 'You can look at this on the minibus,' he said.

When they arrived at the garden centre one of the assistants met them and took them into the café for refreshments. The students were able to put their social skills training into practice and they needed very little prompting.

Before the garden assistant took them round the centre he showed them a large diagram of the layout and explained what they would see. The students looked puzzled. Sam suspected that although they knew what he was saying they weren't capable of applying that knowledge to the plan.

Sam put Jane in charge of the two most capable students and asked Alf, the minibus driver, to join Andy and his partner in case Andy needed any help getting up and down steps. Sam took responsibility for the other two.

The students were encouraged to use the booklets but it was obvious from their reactions they were bored. Sam realised more thought needed to go into them.

After the conducted tour of the gardens the assistant left them to go for his lunch.

The students sat and had their packed lunches on one of the benches. 'We haven't spent our money yet,' said one of them. 'I promised my mum I'd buy her a plant.'

'Right,' said Sam. 'As soon as we've had our lunch we'll see what's for sale.'

Sam encouraged them to ask the garden assistant how to take care of the plants they were buying. This helped develop their skill in communication. Dealing with money presented them with problems. Sam wondered whether he could build this skill into the subject he was teaching them.

By the time Sam saw his head of department the following day he had one or two ideas to suggest to him.

Ray completes his assignment

Ray's students sat in rows in the classroom and when he walked in they took up their pens, adjusted their drawing boards and prepared to copy a diagram either from the board or the overhead projector.

'Put your pens down,' he said. 'We're going to do something completely different today.' He hoped his nervousness didn't show. 'I'm going to split you into groups and you're going to work on an assignment.'

The students were apprehensive.

They formed themselves into three groups and Ray handed out the assignment which read: *Imagine you are a design team that has been commissioned to build an office block and associated facilities on this piece of land.* (There was a diagram of the piece of derelict land indicating its exact position in the town centre.) *Produce a list of points to consider prior to designing the building.*

Ray explained that they were free to ask him for any information they needed.

After a moment's hesitation the students got to work in their groups – each group appointed a member to act as scribe. Conversation buzzed as suggestions were made, considered, rejected and other suggestions made to replace them.

Ray moved around the groups, observing, monitoring, questioning, offering advice and was clearly impressed with the way they were working.

He had allowed 30 minutes on his lesson plan for them to present and discuss their points and for him to make a summary on the overhead projector. The students were eager to argue their reasons for including certain points and leaving out others. Such things as access to the site during construction were considered by all groups – but only two groups had considered access for car parking facilities after completion. The other group argued that space could be more profitably used for the building and staff could park on the multistorey!

Services to the site – gas, electric, water and drainage – were considered by each group, but information was thin on the ground when it came to considering building regulations.

Ray summed up at the end by saying, 'I'm impressed by the way you've worked today. Of course we need to spend a lot more time on this project but you've produced some good ideas. When we've done a bit more work on it I'll arrange for us to go with one of the architects to a building site and he will explain how the design process links in with the construction process.' Ray's enthusiasm for student-centred learning was beginning to show.

'What I'd like you to do before next week,' he said, 'is find out as much as you can about building regulations and then see how they apply to the list you've produced this morning.'

Ray had enjoyed the lesson and his head was buzzing with ideas for future lessons. He hadn't experienced any problems controlling the students – apart from their enthusiasm – and they were still discussing the project amongst themselves as they left to go to their next lesson.

POINTS FOR DISCUSSION

1. What advice would you give to a teacher of your subject who was having problems putting her planning into practice?

2. How might a knowledge of management skills help in the classroom?

3. In what ways is a teacher in control of her class when using student-centred learning?

10
Evaluating Your Teaching

One of your most important tasks as a teacher is to evaluate your teaching. At the end of each lesson you will feel either satisfied that the lesson went well or disheartened because of the problems you experienced. If you felt disheartened the cause may stem from your planning of the lesson.

EXAMINING YOUR PLANNING

Look back at your planning of the lesson and answer the following questions:

- Did you take account of your students' previous knowledge when setting the objectives for the lesson?

- Were you aware of any personal or physical problems that your students were suffering from? If so did you take them into consideration?

- Did you bear in mind the group formations that were taking place and plan work that would encourage the students to break away?

- Was sufficient time allowed to explain and ensure that your students understood new concepts that you were introducing?

- Did you produce resources that aided rather than confused your students?

- Was material planned that would stretch your students to a higher level of learning?

- Did you allow sufficient time for the students to complete each activity?

INTERPRETING FEEDBACK

Once you have checked your planning look carefully at the feedback you received during the lesson. This may help you to identify the reasons for any problems.

Recognising and being able to interpret feedback is something that comes with experience. However, considering the following points may help.

Anxiety in your students
The causes may include:

● An inability to cope with the level of learning – find out their existing level and build on that.

● There may be hostility within the class. Are you spending more time with some students than others? Perhaps 'closed' social groups have formed. Sort out the problem quickly.

● Some may be trying to cope with personal problems that take priority over learning. Talk to them – let them see you are concerned and approachable.

The misinterpretation of information by a student
Perhaps:

● This student is deaf. Arrange for her to sit close to you. Face her as you give information. Provide handouts of key points.

● You used jargon or concepts that were unfamiliar to her. Be aware of the problem and remedy it – simplify your terminology.

● Your presentation of the information was confusing. Rethink your method of teaching.

The inability of your students to keep up with the pace of the lesson
The cause could be:

● You haven't allocated sufficient time at the planning stage of your lesson. Make a note on your lesson plan to allow more time in future.

• Your students are tired. Try to find out the cause. Can you do anything about it? Make your lessons stimulating.

• You have set work that is at a level beyond their capabilities. Back to the drawing board!

Students who are bored
In chapter 2 boredom was listed as one of the reasons for learning being unsuccessful – students 'switch off'. The causes may be:

• Setting your subject material at too low a level. Assess your students' existing capabilities and plan learning at a higher level.

• Giving a boring presentation of your subject. Choose a more stimulating teaching method.

• Repeating parts of the lesson for the benefit of slower learners. Planning group work for the different levels of ability might be the answer.

• They feel they are wasting their time because the course isn't what they expected it to be. Did you discuss the objectives of the course with them at the beginning?

SOURCES OF HELP

Inexperienced teachers may need help with identifying and interpreting feedback in the classroom. There are sources of help that you can turn to, such as the following.

A supervisor
If you are undergoing a teacher training course you will have the benefit of a supervisor to observe your teaching and offer helpful advice.

Video recordings
It may be possible to get the technician from the resource centre to video-record your teaching so that you can view it later. It is surprising the things you notice that you had completely overlooked in the lesson. If you are taking a teacher training course you may be familiar with this technique of providing you with feedback as it is a built-in part of many courses.

Lesson content	strengths	weaknesses	comments
Lesson planning Learning objectives stated. Appropriate teaching methods and resources chosen to aid learning. *Introduction to lesson* Friendly welcome given to students. Objectives of the lesson explained. Interest captured. *Presentation of lesson* Information clearly presented. Resources used effectively. Students actively involved in the lesson. Immediate feedback given to students regarding work and behaviour. Good personal relationships developed. *Assessment of learning* Used a variety of assessment techniques. Used the results of assessment to provide the students with feedback regarding their progress. Gave the feedback in a supportive manner. *Closure of the lesson* Summarised the learning. Recognised a suitable time to close the lesson when time was running short. Praised progress achieved.			

Fig. 15. A chart provides focus for teacher appraisal.

Tape recording

If the above idea is not feasible you can always set up a tape-recorder which will provide you with audio-feedback. But remember to explain the purpose to your students – it could inhibit them if they think you are using it for sinister means!

A colleague

It can be useful to ask a colleague, preferably one who teaches the same subject as you, to sit in on one of your lessons and then discuss it with you afterwards. However, you need to make it clear to her that you are looking for constructive criticism and not just a general remark such as 'It was very enjoyable' or 'It wasn't bad.'

Your colleague, of course, must be capable of offering constructive criticism. A chart such as that in Figure 15 would provide a focus for appraisal. It would be useful to discuss it with her before the observation – stressing that you would like her to comment on your strengths and weaknesses in each of the areas.

WHAT ARE YOUR STRENGTHS?

Remember that feedback can highlight your strengths as well as your weaknesses.

Teaching strengths

You will be able to judge your strengths by:

- Listening to what your students say. Mature students will let you know if they are enjoying your lessons.

- Watching what your students do. If they are coping with the learning and produce good results you have probably pitched the lesson at the right level for them.

- Noticing whether the students appreciate the concern you show and the practical help you give to the ones with physical or personal problems. Once they see that you can be trusted and are approachable they will settle down to learn knowing that they can rely on your support.

- Observing whether your lesson runs like clockwork. If it does you probably have the ability to recognise when to move your students from one activity to the next – governed by their achievements –

or recognise when to change your planned lesson if it isn't working.

Once you have considered your strengths and weaknesses you need to consider any changes that need to be made.

RINGING THE CHANGES

Your job as a teacher needs to be changing all the time in response to feedback. Feedback that highlights your strengths will provide you with a positive self-image. However, it pays not to be complacent: sticking to what you know just because it's tried and tested may soon lead to your students becoming bored. Be prepared to:

* experiment
* be innovative
* keep abreast of your subject
* attend updating courses
* involve your students in decision-making.

Ignore colleagues who are cynical and think that students should be kept in their place and only you should make the decisions.

Mature students need to be treated as mature people. They have a wealth of experiences which, if appropriate, you should draw on. This gives them a feeling of worth and helps produce interesting and lively lessons ensuring that your students are keen to attend your classes.

If the feedback highlights your weaknesses then changes need to be made early on in the course, before the problems fester and your students start to drift away.

Take a good look at the rules for learning in chapter 3. Are there any that you are not putting into practice?

In chapter 2 the factors that hinder learning were considered. Are you guilty of any of them?

If you are unable to make changes without help then seek it soon.

CASE STUDIES

Sarah's supervisor provides her with feedback

'How do you feel now that you've had time to reflect on the lesson?' asked the supervisor as Sarah joined her in the tutorial room.

'I thought it went quite well.'

'On the whole,' said the supervisor, 'you seem to be putting into practice what you've learned on your training course. I was particularly impressed with the light-hearted way in which you introduced the lesson – it dispelled any nervousness they had about me.'

'I was surprised at how the students went out of their way to be supportive – more so than usual,' said Sarah.

'That's because I was there. This usually happens. It's their way of telling me, *We think she's good so don't knock her.*'

Sarah smiled. 'I've made a few notes on my appraisal form,' she said. 'I feel there are one or two areas that need looking at.'

'It's always a good idea to reflect on the lesson and make your own appraisal before we have a tutorial,' said the supervisor. 'After all once you've finished your training course you're on your own – so you must be able to pinpoint any weaknesses that you may have and produce remedies for them. What comments have you made?'

'The slides, I thought, were a good idea even though it threw me a little when one was upside down.'

'It wasn't a major problem and you dealt with it well. You need a sense of humour if you're going to succeed in the teaching profession.'

'I was surprised at the amount of interest shown in them – at one stage I couldn't make myself heard over the babble.'

'How might you have coped with this?' asked the supervisor.

Sarah thought for a moment. 'By stopping talking myself?'

'Yes. Or you could have said something like, *This slide is of a design I thought we might work on next week – I'll draw the stages on the board for you.*'

'Because this was something they all needed to know for next week you would probably have got their attention – especially as you were drawing on the board. Diagrams that develop before their eyes usually intrigue.'

'Yes, I've noticed that,' said Sarah. 'On reflection I think I showed too many slides – it threw my timing. I was grateful that a student reminded me of the cake in the oven.'

'That was another indication of your students protecting you from me,' said the supervisor. 'She didn't want you to produce a burnt cake while you were being observed.'

'Because I was running short of time I felt I rushed the closure of the lesson.'

'Yes, but timing comes with experience. You seem only to be telling me about your weaknesses, what about your strengths?'

'I felt I was well prepared,' said Sarah. 'And the atmosphere in the classroom was relaxed and friendly.'

'Yes. And don't forget your sense of humour. You displayed just the right amount. Too much humour in a lesson can become boring. You did very well. I enjoyed your lesson.'

Sarah went away thinking how far she had come since that first disastrous lesson which led to the loss of her class.

Sam considers how to improve future visits

'How did the visit go?' the head of department asked Sam the following morning.

'Fine. I learned a lot about the students.'

'Yes, it's surprising how much more you learn about their capabilities when you get them out of their usual teaching situation,' said the head. 'How were their social skills?'

'They had plenty of opportunities to put them into practice – in the café and the shop – but they struggled a bit paying for the plants. I thought what I would do before we go again is pot up a few plants in the greenhouse and they can sell them to the staff. It will give them some practice at handling money.'

'That's a good idea,' said the head.

'The booklets I produced weren't very successful,' said Sam. 'The lads got despondent when they couldn't find some of the plants. I should have made a visit first before taking them. This would have given me a better idea of what to expect and then my planning would have been more appropriate.'

'Mm. What would you change?' asked the head.

'Well, my idea was to give them something to do so that they wouldn't be walking around aimlessly. On reflection a better idea would be to get a copy of the layout of the garden centre and then produce some handouts so that they could have a copy each to follow on the next visit. I'd need to do some work with them on it first because most of them looked confused when the assistant tried to explain it to them.'

'I'm not surprised,' said the head.

'For the ones who can't read I could include some diagrams to indicate the greenhouse area, pond, fruit trees . . .'

'That's a good idea,' interrupted the head. 'You could even get them to draw some of the diagrams. Helping to produce the plans would act as a motivator to use them.'

'It's a job for a rainy day,' said Sam. 'It's always difficult to know what to do with them when the weather's bad.'

The visit had made Sam realise that preparation is important and it needs to be made with the capabilities of the learners in mind. His decision to familiarise the students with the layout of the garden centre will ensure that they have some starting knowledge to build on next time they visit.

Ray evaluates his lesson

'How did it go?' Ray's colleague asked the day after he had taught his assignment lesson.

'Great. No problem. I really enjoyed it.'

'Said you would, didn't I?'

'I have to do an appraisal of it now and hand it in to my tutor with the lesson plan,' Ray told him. 'We have an appraisal chart to remind us of the various components of a lesson.'

Ray was amazed when he looked at his strengths and weaknesses at how successful the lesson had been. He had covered all the points in the planning and his presentation of the lesson had more strengths than weaknesses. After making what he thought was a fairly accurate appraisal, he handed it to his tutor.

A few days later he saw his tutor for the feedback.

'Well, Ray, from your lesson planning and appraisal it seems as though it was a successful assignment.'

'I was surprised at how well it went,' said Ray.

'Good. Tell me about it.'

Ray looked at his copy of the appraisal chart for a minute and then said, 'I felt I'd planned it adequately bearing in mind the objective of the lesson . . .'

'Which was?' his tutor interrupted.

'That the students should discuss in groups the assignment I gave them and produce a list of points to be considered prior to designing a building – the points to be presented to the rest of the class.'

'Right,' said his tutor.

'On reflection I should have allowed more time for them to present their lists and I could have collected the information in a different way.'

'How?' asked the tutor.

'Well, as each group had made similar points I could have taken the same point from each group and discussed it rather than asking each group to present their lists separately – there was a lot of overlap, which was time wasting.'

'The ability to recognise and change ineffective presentation in the lesson comes with experience – but it seems to me that you are beginning to think along the right lines.'

Ray went on to discuss the rest of the lesson with his tutor who was impressed with the way he had tackled his appraisal. 'I know you've been reluctant to accept student-centred learning, haven't you Ray?' he said. 'But from your appraisal it sounds as though you enjoyed this lesson.'

'I did. I have to admit I wasn't looking forward to it. I always felt that the teacher should be in charge.'

'But you were in charge. From what you've told me you controlled the students' learning very well. By adopting this method you've provided yourself with information about their existing knowledge. And by setting the task of finding out about building regulations you are encouraging them in research techniques – allowing them to find out for themselves. Always guide. Don't tell. Act as a resource person. I must say I'm looking forward to observing one of your lessons.'

At last Ray was beginning to see teaching as something more than just passing on information.

POINTS FOR DISCUSSION

1. What are the main points to consider when evaluating your teaching?

2. The success of teaching is measured by the success of the students' learning. What advice would you give to a teacher who was failing in the classroom?

3. Of what value is feedback (a) to the student, (b) to the teacher?

Glossary

Accountability. Being responsible for actions. A teacher is accountable to her students particularly in the area of assessment where she has to justify marks or grades given. It is important, therefore, to have an objective marking scheme.

Affective. This term relates to feelings and attitudes. Feelings of satisfaction, enjoyment, anxiety or distress will all affect the student's motivation to learn.

Analysis. The breaking down of a task in order to identify the skills involved.

Assessment. A process of estimating whether the learning objectives have been achieved. Ongoing assessment providing immediate feedback about the students' progress is preferable to one end of term examination that might catch a student on an 'off day'. It is advisable to use a range of methods that will test at various levels of learning.

Cognitive environment. A learning situation in which the interplay of the teacher's and student's mental processes takes place. The teacher must have a mental awareness of the students' mental preparedness for the new learning.

Cognitive skills. Those abilities that are brought about by the mental functioning of the brain. They enable students to latch new information on to their existing knowledge and use it to explain new situations. Skills such as those involved in problem-solving.

Communication. A means of transmitting and receiving information. For learning to take place the teacher must ensure that the message she is transmitting is being received and understood by the students. She must also receive and understand the feedback she is getting from her students.

Concepts. Classes of objects or events that are either concrete or abstract. Concrete concepts such as 'desk', 'table' or 'chalkboard' are easy to learn because they can be seen. Abstract concepts such as 'leisure' or 'progress' are much more difficult to learn –

we can't point to a 'leisure' or a 'progress' – and so students have to be given experience of them in use.

Counsellor. A person, usually a member of the teaching staff, who has been trained and appointed to listen to a student's problem and then guide and support the student towards solving the problem in her own way.

Evaluation of teaching. The activity of looking at the process of teaching and measuring its success in terms of the students' learning. It enables a teacher to identify her strengths and weaknesses from the feedback she receives in the classroom and to consider whether to make changes.

Feedback. The information being received by students and teacher about activities taking place in the classroom. Students receive feedback about their performance from (a) the teacher (b) other students who discuss it with them and (c) from the job in hand *eg* if the cement doesn't set the bricklaying student knows he needs to check the mixture. The teacher receives feedback from the students about the success of her teaching.

Learning. This is a change in behaviour (what a person can do) brought about as a result of experience. A great deal of learning takes place incidentally, that is to say without the person making a conscious effort to learn. A child will learn to walk when he is physically ready. An adult will learn how to behave in certain situations by being exposed to those situations.

Learning objectives. Exact statements of what the students should achieve after a period of teaching. The classroom activities should be planned with the specific learning objectives in mind.

Motivation. An emotional state that drives a student to engage in activities that fulfil a need such as learning in order to gain qualifications. The teacher needs to keep this motivation stimulated by providing feedback to ensure the student develops a positive self-image. This will in turn maintain the motivation.

Motor skills. Those skills that require the use of the limbs. For example in writing, the motor skills involved are holding the pen, moving the hand to form the letters and gliding the pen from left to right.

Multiple-choice objective tests. Tests that require the student to choose one answer from a selection given. They do not have to express themselves in writing and they are at liberty to guess the answer. There must be one right answer only but the others must be plausible. Anyone can mark the tests given the appropriate marking scheme and often they are marked by computer.

However, they need to be compiled by experts in order to ensure that they are testing exactly what they are supposed to be testing.

Note-making. Unlike note-taking the student is required to concentrate on the information being presented, attempt to understand it and then condense it into note form for future reference. Notes may be made in linear form, columnar form or in patterns.

Note-taking. A method of copying information from a board, a book or the overhead projector or writing notes verbatim from dictation by the teacher. It does not require the student to understand the information being written.

Objective assessment. Assessment of the situation as it really is – uncoloured by feelings or emotions. Personal values and opinions should not be allowed to cloud judgement when marking students' work. It is important therefore to have an objective marking scheme.

Psychomotor skills. Skills that involve perception plus muscular activities. The muscular activities (motor skills) of lifting the arm, flicking the wrist, stepping forward that are so often required when learning physical tasks are useless unless the learner also perceives why he is doing it, how to get from one stage to the next, what the task should look like when it is complete and so on.

Physical environment. The surroundings in which the lesson takes place such as the arrangement of tables, desks, chairs, position of electrical sockets, chalkboard and so on. These need to be taken into consideration when planning the lesson.

Reinforcement. This is the term used to describe events that increase the probability of an activity being repeated. For example if a student receives praise from the teacher for arriving early it is likely that she will continue to arrive early. It is said that the behaviour (of arriving early) is being reinforced.

Resources. Aids used to support teaching and learning. They range from the simplest handout to the most sophisticated computer software and should be chosen or designed with the learning objectives in mind.

Rote-learning. Memorising information by repetition such as learning poetry or number-tables parrot fashion. The information does not necessarily have meaning for the learner.

Scheme of work. The teacher's personal interpretation of the syllabus which she has broken down into sections that can be taught within an allotted time. Each section usually constitutes a topic and it is important that the topics are organised on the scheme of work so that the students are introduced to the simple tasks before the complex.

Skills. Those parts of a task that have been identified by analysing it into its component parts. For example, the task of using a dictionary has many skills both motor and cognitive (thinking). The motor skills of holding the dictionary and sorting through the pages are combined with the cognitive skills of knowing the alphabet, finding the page, recognising the word and then understanding the definition given.

Social environment. The social and personal interactions of the teacher and the students that take place within the classroom. If the relationships are harmonious they can work to the good of the group by removing the anxiety that will inhibit learning.

Stage specimen. A resource often used by teachers of practical subjects to illustrate the stages that go into the making of the finished product. The various stages of producing a joint in woodwork or a blouse in dressmaking can be shown. However, they are not meant to replace the teacher's demonstration of the skill but are useful for the students to handle and inspect.

Student-centred learning. Learning that requires the student to be actively involved rather than passively listening to the teacher. The teacher sets up appropriate conditions for the learning to take place and then acts as a manager and resource person, monitoring, advising and supporting whenever necessary.

Study skills. Skills required by the students to help them to study effectively. They include note-making skills, speed reading, essay writing, revision skills and so on.

Syllabus. A list of topics to be covered during a course, produced by either an external examining board or the course organiser. It doesn't usually indicate the relative importance of the topics or the order in which they are to be studied – this is the job of the teacher when she draws up her scheme of work.

Teacher-centred learning. The teacher is in complete control of the learning situation. She makes all the decisions and does not allow the students to think for themselves. Much of the learning may be rote-learning and result in the students failing to understand and therefore unable to apply the knowledge.

Team teaching. A term used to describe a group of teachers and specialist staff who carry out the administration and or teaching or a course.

Transfer of learning. The carrying forward of learned skills to new situations *eg* the ability to type can be transferred when using a word processor.

Further Reading

How to Study: A practical guide, Francis Casey (Macmillan Education, 1986). Deals with the simple technique of how to approach and organise study.

Adult Study Tactics: A springboard to learning, Diana Percy (Macmillan: Australia, 1989). A practical handbook to guide the reader through the pitfalls and pressures of studying.

How to Succeed in Exams and Assessments, Penny Henderson (Collins Educational, 1993). Designed to help develop skills in all kinds of assessment.

The Assessment of Performance and Competence – a handbook for teachers and trainers, L. Walkin (Stanley Thornes [Publishers] 1991). A practical guide to planning, teaching and assessing activities.

Teaching and Learning in Further and Adult Education L. Walkin (Stanley Thornes [Publishers] 1990). An aid to teachers in further education and trainers in industry and commerce who wish to gain a new qualification or update their skills.

Teaching Adults, Alan Rogers (Open University Press,1992). Useful for lecturers, tutors, instructors or trainers, health visitors and clergy.

Developing Courses for Students, Derek Rowntree (Paul Chapman Publishing 1981). Written for teachers in post-secondary education who are producing courses.

Producing Teaching Materials – a handbook for teachers and trainers, Henry Ellington and Phil Race (Kogan Page, 1993). A survey manual on how to make teaching materials.

Teaching Skills in Further and Adult Education, David Minton (City & Guilds/Macmillan, 1991). Suitable for students on the City & Guilds Further and Adult Education Teacher's Certificate Course.

Teaching Basic Skills to Adults with Learning Difficulties, (NIACE – National Organisation for Adult Learners, 1994). This book is aimed at people new to teaching basic skills to adults with learning difficulties.

A Guide to Student-Centred Learning, Donna Brandes and Paul Ginnis (Simons & Schuster Education, 1993). The emphasis is on activity-based learning and teacher-student collaboration rather than on teaching and instruction.

Teaching in Further Education, Trevor Kerry and Janice Tollitt-Evans (Blackwell, 1992). A practical, classroom approach to teaching in further education.

Adults Learning (3rd edition), Jenny Rogers (Open University Press, 1992). Practical down-to-earth advice on all the common problems of helping adults learn.

How to Study and Learn: Your Practical Guide to Effective Study Skills, Peter Marshall (How To Books, 1995).

Training Courses Available

Some of the following courses require you to be teaching adults part-time or full-time or alternatively have access to adults being trained or assessed. If your local college offers the course they will be able to tell you the entry requirements or provide you with addresses or telephone numbers to contact for the details.

Further and Adult Education Teachers' Certificate (C&G 730–7)

Certificate in Continuing Professional Development – Special Needs (C&G 740–1)

Certificate in Adult, Further and Higher Education

Professional Training for Adult Basic Education (C&G 9285)

RSA/UCLES Diploma in Teaching English as a Foreign Language

NVQ Level 3 Training and Development

Skills Assessor (C&G TDLB D32)

Vocational Assessor (C&G TDLB D33)

Index